7 May 2019

D0230576

Two Turtle Doves

A Memoir of Making Things

Alex Monroe

BLOOMSBURY

LONDON • NEW DELHI • NEW YORK • SYDNEY

First published in Great Britain 2014
This paperback edition published 2015

Text copyright © 2014 by Alex Monroe
Illustrations and photographs copyright © 2014 by Alex Monroe, except illustrations on
pages 1, 30, 54, 74, 99, 122, 149, 176, 204 and 227 by Holly Macdonald
Photograph on page 47 copyright © Ben Rice (benrice.com)
Photograph on page 177 copyright © David Stockings

The author and publishers would like to thank Sham 69 for permission to include on page 65
lyrics from 'Hersham Boys' co-written by Jimmy Pursey and Dave Parsons. Epigraph on page vii
is taken from *Swallowdale* by Arthur Ransome. Published by Jonathan Cape. Reprinted by
permission of The Random House Group Limited. US rights reprinted by permission of David
R. Godine, Publisher, Inc. Copyright © 1931 by Arthur Ransome. Quotation on page 11 taken
from *Swallows and Amazons* by Arthur Ransome. Published by Jonathan Cape. Reprinted by
permission of The Random House Group Limited. US rights reprinted by permission of David
R. Godine, Publisher, Inc. Copyright © 1930 by Arthur Ransome

Every reasonable effort has been made to trace copyright holders of material
reproduced in this book, but if any have been inadvertently overlooked, the
publishers would be glad to hear from them

Bloomsbury Publishing plc
50 Bedford Square
London
WC1B 3DP
www.bloomsbury.com

Bloomsbury is a trademark of Bloomsbury Publishing Plc

Bloomsbury Publishing, London, New Delhi, New York and Sydney

A CIP catalogue record for this book is available from the British Library

ISBN 978 1 4088 4120 4
10 9 8 7 6 5 4 3 2 1

Typeset by Hewer Text UK Ltd, Edinburgh

Printed and bound in Great Britain by CPI Group (UK) Ltd, Croydon CR0 4YY

MIX
Paper from
responsible sources
FSC® C020471

For Denise, Very, Con and the Lobster

When a thing's done, it's done, and if it's not done right,
do it differently next time.

Arthur Ransome, *Swallowdale*, 1931

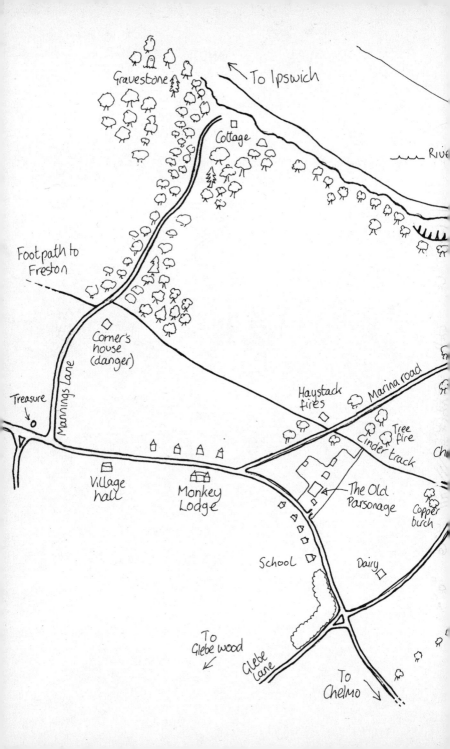

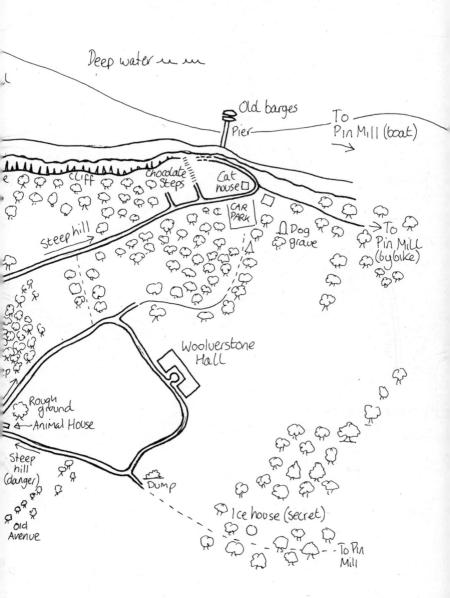

WOOLVERSTONE AND THE RIVER ORWELL

Deep water

Old barges

Pier

To Pin Mill (boat)

Cliff

Chocolate Steps

Cat house

CAR PARK

Steep hill

Dog grave

To Pin Mill (by bike)

Woolverstone Hall

Rough ground

Animal House

Steep hill (danger)

Dump

Ice house (secret)

Old Avenue

To Pin Mill

Chrysanthemum

I'm squinting as I emerge from the Metro station. It's March so the sun is bright and low, glancing off the sandstone walls of the Tuileries' austere gardens. Bare trees and classical sculptures throw long shadows across pale gravelled paths. The traffic in the Rue de Rivoli behind me is as noisy as ever and the Musée d'Orsay tempts from the opposite bank of the Seine. A waft of cigarette smoke mingles with the fresh air and scent of sun on stone.

Parallel with road and river, long white marquees run the entire length of this vast space. Already I'm noticing a ridiculous number of skinny women dressed in black. They stand posturing in groups, sunglasses huge, cigarettes in one hand, phone in the other, their hair expensively dyed in streaks and pulled up tight. Their faces are pulled tight too, giving a harshness that's hard to put your finger on at first. It's a kind of blankness, which makes me think, as I look closer, that they've had some work done. They all sport big black shoulder bags, bright lipstick and shiny hoop earrings – just a little glint of bling is allowed. This is the uniform of The Fashion Buyer.

We're in Paris for Fashion Week. Twice a year, March and September, designers come to show, the press comes to write and buyers come to buy. It's a mad rush from season to season, show to show, collection to collection. Time slips away unnoticed while the months are measured out in marquees. This must be my twentieth year in Paris. I exhibit each year in London and Tokyo as well, New York if I've got the energy, and from time to time Berlin and Melbourne too, unveiling a new collection of forty or so themed pieces: necklaces on lavish and modest scales, a selection of earrings, some rings and a few bracelets. The pressure is to second-guess – or better still, inspire – the following season's 'new look'.

Down the steps, a doorman in a bright yellow puffer jacket lets me in and after a flash of my security pass, I'm swallowed up by the first tent: *Paris Sur Môde*.

The white space inside is divided into booths, monochrome settings for rack after rack of new clothes. The air is warm and sugary with the smell of sweet coffee mixed with a hundred different perfumes. Subdued and sophisticated muzak loops under the chatter, its hint of Europop echoing the medley of languages and accents I catch as I pass – there's Russian, French, Italian, American and Japanese too, of course. These visitors are also all in black. Footsteps are muffled but not silenced by the carpet covering the wooden flooring. Some people stomp purposefully down the aisle, while others totter along in shoes as unfeasibly high as they're fashionable. My own uniform of jeans and trainers comes from years of experience and a longing for comfort.

As a rule, buyers move in packs. The Japanese tend to trawl the shows in groups of five or six. There's a gang of them coming along now: three men (the bosses, no doubt – the money men) and two exhausted-looking women who'll be making the decisions. Italians move in threes, British buyers seem to operate mostly in twos, while big American stores roam in threes or fours. They pull things off racks and wreck elegant displays with nonchalance. Their silhouettes widen as they progress, great shiny bags multiplying on arms and shoulders.

I've made it through *Paris Sur Môde* and I'm into *Première Classe* now. The difference is striking. It's more cramped and busy here, and smells much sweatier too. It's horribly hot. In the old days you couldn't see from one end to the other for the cigarette smoke. *Paris Sur Môde* is clothes; *Première Classe* is accessories. One of several such shows in Paris, it's both the biggest and the toughest to get into. The organisers have a strict selection process and it shows.

There's more variety here in people as well as products. There goes a guy in skinny purple jeans and yellow shoes, tossing his orange ponytail. He looks as though he's got a monkey strapped to his back but it's just the fur lining of his jacket. A tall and beautiful black man with short-cropped peroxided hair and a seventies pornstar moustache is wearing an ankle-length dress of floating purple under his leather jacket and stiletto boots with fur pompoms. I think of the streets around my studio in Elephant and Castle and wonder how long he'd last there.

There's a real mix of things on show too: shoes, bags, scarves, belts and, of course, jewellery, which itself varies from huge dinner-plate-sized necklaces to pieces precious in their detail, set with minute gems or intricately filigreed. We're at the nuts-and-bolts end of the international fashion industry here, all business and hard work. It's an absolute meritocracy that's upfront and honest, but it comes with hard knocks, too. If your stuff sells, you survive. If it doesn't, you won't last two minutes. That's why I like it here. And why it makes me nervous.

Weaving towards my own stand, my eye is briefly caught by a display of gigantic necklaces of pearls and beads hung on coat hangers. American. They're good at this, these three pretty young women with big hair and big smiles. I've caught their eye now . . . *Hi, how are you?* One approaches with a clipboard. *I'm an exhibitor,* I say. Her smile drops and she's off in a millisecond. Good for her. No point in making small talk with me. I move on past an Italian company with loud plastic necklaces selling to a group of older women, beautiful long white hair hanging down their black dresses. Opposite, a Japanese designer has a wonderful display made entirely of paper, tiny gold pieces glistening with micro-set diamonds. But no buyers, so the two young Japanese women sit and chat at the table, holding their mobile phones. Next there's a collection of vast mirrored pieces that catch the lights and dazzle me as I pass.

And then it's me.

My stand looks scruffy in contrast, and it smells of burning wood. I've made lamps for the occasion out of Suffolk twigs, but the hazel wands are overheating, and the hot bulbs seem to scorch the bark. I worry a little about the fragile twists of smoke that rise from time to time (you'd never get away with this in London) but I love the reminder of autumn. Bonfires and incense. If I get it right today, that's when this jewellery should be in the shops. Chrysanthemum season.

Chrysanthemum is the name of this collection. I haven't put the whole lot out on the front plinth. Instead I've made a simple arrangement of key pieces, each necklace or pair of earrings lying on its own Perspex block, which is lit from within. They're designed as tempting tasters to lead buyers to the display tray at the back of the stand, where the rest of the collection waits for judgement. Gold stands out best on the blocks' translucent white tops, so these are the pieces I've chosen for the front, and unusually, this particular collection is looking just a bit sparkly.

There's an asymmetric necklace here with pea-sized white pearls strung on one side, and a large blooming chrysanthemum flower in the middle. An organic bud-like setting holds it in place with leaves and a single pearl. The cocktail ring is as big as I've ever made: three flowers burst into life, almost blousy as they jostle for space. Of the three different pairs of earrings, the most glamorous are the smallest: pearl and faceted white topaz. Tiny flower buds have tinier diamonds set at their centre, and another pair borrows the pattern of chrysanthemum leaves, their stems forming elegant ear-hooks, their surface softened by flick-brushing to imitate the sheen of their pearls. I've used black pearls too, at the heart of a couple of iridescent raven-black blooms, an effect achieved by ruthenium electroplated over gold over silver. The black pieces won't sell as well as the gold and silver, but they're fun and attention-grabbing and that's just as important here.

There's no time to eat. Just as you're about to tidy away the debris of coffee cups, someone else is inspecting the stand, asking what it's all about this time. You always need a line on the latest collection: a snappy PR quote that will feed the buzz. This time it's easy, because I knew right from the start what I was after. It's pure Grace Kelly, a new take on classic 1950s glamour. Form and texture; gold and pearls. An antidote to the looming financial crisis, I hope.

That's the quick answer. But of course there's more to every collection than a headline, and never time in a rushed fashion-show exchange to go back to the beginning and get a sense of where it all started. Sometimes I haven't quite worked it out for myself. Like the forgotten source of an estuary – widening as it reaches the sea, repeatedly returning on itself with the tides, carrying silt and gathering debris, washing over the same territory but always changing – the origins of a piece of jewellery can be obscured even to its maker. I've made things for as long as I can remember (go-carts and necklaces, ammunition and earrings, bicycles and bracelets) but it's taken me till now to start to map the tributaries of ideas and memories, and the flow of people and emotions running between these different creations.

Few of my collections have more distant headwaters than the little pieces that now lie glittering under the smoking lights at *Première Classe*. Chrysanthemums were significant in my family history well before I was born. In my childhood though, it was their absence that made them distinctive.

My mother, Peggy-Ann, was a wonderfully keen gardener but chrysanthemums were one of the few flowers she couldn't bear. *Great big blousy fellows,* she would say. Very non-U. Some of the villagers grew them in their pretty bright cottage gardens, vibrant splashes of vivid colour among the veg and the red-hot pokers. I thought they looked splendid, and so they did, but I quickly learned they wouldn't 'do' for us. They would have looked out of place beside our apricot and almond trees, and subtle swathes of ferns and grasses set against elegantly curving walls and lawns.

What I didn't realise then was that my mother had a history with chrysanthemums.

5

Her father had absolutely adored them. They were his life's great passion. In fact, I wonder if he mightn't have loved the flowers more than he loved anything else. But at that age I never actually thought to wonder if my mother even had a father. He wasn't ever talked about, and it didn't occur to me to poke around. It's only as I piece together the family history now, following trails of words and paper and images into the past, hints of stories trailing through time, that I begin to see how the past plays out in the work I do today.

My mother turned six in the summer of 1937, and her family lived in Lytham St Annes, the posh side of Preston, in a respectably large Victorian end-of-terrace. She remembers a red-brick façade with a shiny black front door, stone pillars on the bay window and white-painted sash windows.

When I quiz her, she tells me that her father Charles was one of twelve children, all Devon-born, and she uses the word 'uneasy' to describe him. As soon as he could, Charles ran away to Canada, where he married and had a son called John. Canada was not a success. His first wife promptly died and work was certainly not worth staying for. Charles came back to London with his son and he seems to have met and begun courting my grandmother, Madeleine, almost immediately.

Madeleine was everything that Charles was not: young, beautiful, intelligent and posh. She might also have been more than a little naive. I can't help assuming this from her convent education. In the early 1900s she happily shared a dorm at St Ursula's Convent School in Greenwich with a delightful mix of French, German and Norwegian girls. The school had been founded in 1877 by German nuns expelled from the Empire when Bismarck's grip on state education tightened. By the time Madeleine became a boarder, most of the German sisters had returned home, and teaching had been largely taken over by French nuns escaping their own government's increasingly anti-Catholic stance. It's hard to imagine that these sheltered sisters and their motto of *Poverty, Chastity and Obedience* were the best preparation for a young woman in matters of love.

When Charles was presented to Madeleine's parents, they took an immediate dislike to him. He had overdressed in an effort to impress: plus fours and, reportedly, a rather silly moustache, which was lacquered down and shiny, like his hair. He came across as a bad imitation of a country squire, sweating uncomfortably in an inappropriately stiff collar. Much older than Madeleine, brash and slightly spivvy, Charles was painfully aware that her parents saw straight through him. I suppose they were trained to do just that. Maddy's mother was French and a *grande dame* of the old order. They lived a grand life in a grand house in Berkshire, where everything they consumed was ordered down from Harrods and delivered in the shop's conspicuous green van. Peggy-Ann particularly remembers the weekly arrival of the Harrods' library van. Even the family's reading matter had to come from the right place.

Against her parents' wishes, Madeleine and Charles were married. Charles got a job in manufacturing (imagine!) and they moved to Preston. Awkward and out of his depth, Charles quickly ran into difficulties at the firm. Work went no better when he left to start his own business. It had something to do with cereals, connected to his time in Canada, perhaps. By this point Madeleine seems to have lost her naivety, and stepped into the breach left by her husband's inadequacies.

At least there was one place where Charles could escape, and one thing he could do well. At the back of the house was a long thin garden full of roses and flower beds. There was also a large greenhouse and a potting shed. The greenhouse was a blaze of colour. A jumble of crimson and salmon, yellow and orange, chestnut, gold and terracotta. It was full of chrysanthemums. I imagine him opening the glass door and inhaling a scent of earth and concentrated florist – green, grassy, fresh but not floral. Did his breathing become slower as he inspected plants for crown buds, and did his muscles relax as he pinched off the 'first break' of a promising-looking pompom?

For several years running Charles had won gold at the Lytham St Annes' horticultural show and a number of his blooms had shone in regional competitions too. Here was a place where gaudy was good. In fact, the bigger and brighter, the better. There was no need for pretence or subtlety or feigned sophistication in the world of competitive chrysanthemum-growing.

And the 1930s were exciting times for a cultivator of exhibition-standard flowers. Whole new varieties of chrysanthemum were springing to life each year – Japanese and large anemone, reflexed and incurved, double garden and pot singles. Strings of married women, like Mrs W. Jinks, Mrs Barkley, or Mrs F. Coster, gave their names to new blooms in lavender and blush, purple and amaranth, tangerine and mauve. Breeders developed flowers with eye-catching multi-coloured petals, showy and superior, with grandiose names to match. The Marquis of Northampton was buff, suffused with rose. The Duchess of Fife stood tall in white with lilac streaks and pink. Lady Conyers boasted a silvery reverse. The gaudier types had brasher names. Tuxedo was bronze, Money Maker and Market Gold simply white and yellow. There was even a variety called Freedom.

Out of the way in his outhouses, Charles could lose himself in a sea of colour. Colour and sound. For Charles also loved Wagner. He spent all his free time pampering his beloved blooms and playing Wagner, far too loud.

It wasn't often that he had much to do with any of his children. When my uncle Bill was born in 1935, his half-brother John was already eighteen and working in London. Occasionally though, on a Saturday evening, Peggy-Ann remembers Charles finishing early in his potting shed. Coming into the house, he'd feign a great intrigue with his daughter, and she happily played along with it. In this mood he called her Topsy.

I have a surprise for you, Topsy, he would announce. *I think, Topsy, we will cook supper tonight. Just the two of us! What do you think about that?*

As if this were the most extraordinary surprise. As if it had never happened before.

Then he would head over to the gramophone, pull out a heavy disc from its brown-paper sleeve, and turn the volume up a little more until Wagner was resounding through every room in the house. Together they would fry the week's leftover bacon rind (cooks' perks) until it was nice and crispy. And into the melted-down bacony fat, he'd throw in a couple of floured and seasoned herrings. The surprise was always a herring supper, served with neat slices of buttered bread, and a cup of tea. It was eaten in the cold, dark and dusty dining room to music played at such a volume that there was no chance at all of conversation. Charles sat at the head of the table dressed like a country squire, lost in his Wagner, while his small daughter quietly ate. There was never any mention of the fact that the family's finances were slowly slipping away.

One particular evening though there would be no bacon and no herring surprise for Topsy. It was early September now. The day had been hot and close, and the early exhibition chrysanthemums were just coming into bloom. The back door of the house stood open and *Lohengrin* came booming from inside, even more loudly than usual, so the music could be heard clearly right through the garden. The roses were still flowering and beds of the hardier chrysanthemums overflowed, spilling out onto the lawn. Their great petalled heads dipped and drooped over the grass, too heavy for their stalks to bear.

The roof and one side of the greenhouse had been whitewashed to protect the plants from an excess of sun, but the colour inside was intense enough to blaze through the opaque glass. The greenhouse vents and door were wide open. Nothing unusual about that after a warm and sultry day. But the door to the potting shed was closed.

The shed had a small overgrown window, too dirty to see through, but all the family knew what lay inside. A workbench ran down one side, covered with a jumble of pots and tools, while more trowels and scissors and secateurs hung on the wall behind, alongside coils of string and carefully saved oddments of wire. Another wall was almost

9

entirely papered with certificates, faded rosettes, and photographs of Charles at the height of his success, accepting his prizes. Wooden trays and buckets of soil stood on the floor. (*A herring box is a capital thing for cuttings*, reads a guide to *The Culture of the Chrysanthemum*, published in 1920.) A large bundle of blooms past their best were piled down one end of the bench, their petals browning but their colour still vibrant. At the far end, an old bookcase was crammed with bottles, tins and jam jars, labels beginning to curl.

In the competitive world of the flower show, every grower was naturally armed with an array of potions and powders, fertilisers, fungicides and insecticides. You had to be alert at all times to stem rot or leaf spot, verticillium wilt, rust, powdery mildew, thrips, capsids and red spider mite. Of course this was long before anyone worried about being organic or eco-friendly. Ammonia and copper sulphate were hardly unusual in a suburban potting shed, while one of the most common treatments for leaf nematodes was a double-strength spray of nicotine sulphate and Bordeaux Mixture.

Beside the shelves of chemicals was a chair. A Lloyd Loom that had become too tatty for the house, perhaps, or a wood-and-canvas folding contraption, with arms? I'm not sure. But I'm told that on this particular September evening, when the sun was still out but no longer on the lawn, in this chair sat Charles. He was slumped as if asleep, his head on one side. The kind of neck-cricking slump from which you wake up stiff and aching. There was a small stool beside him, on which stood an empty whisky bottle and a glass. But Charles wasn't snoozing. Charles would never wake up. From inside the house *Lohengrin* churned on.

Death by poisoning reads the death certificate. Accident or suicide? I can't help wondering if it could even have been something more sinister. It sounds so like a scenario from a Miss Marple mystery. But I shy away from these thoughts. My mother remembers that he kept his nicotine solution in an old whisky bottle. It was something gardeners often made themselves, a treacherous infusion of tobacco acting on the nerves of insects and humans alike, potentially more powerful than either arsenic or strychnine. Hardly a pleasant way to die. Confusion is one of the first symptoms. If he realised his mistake, he may have been in no condition to call for help. Seizures and coma are quickly followed by respiratory arrest.

However the poison may have found its way into the glass, the family suddenly found itself destitute and homeless, with little in the way of life insurance to compensate. I'm not sure that they were overly bereft though. Two years after his death, war broke out in Europe. There were other things to worry about.

The nuns had actually done their job rather well after all. Unlike her husband, Madeleine was both accomplished and extremely resourceful. After a stint teaching French and piano at Wellington College, she moved her family to Scotland, where she had secured the post of governess to the Molteno family in Fortingall in Perthshire. She had six Molteno children in her charge, and two of her own, and they all lived in a sprawling seventeenth-century mansion remodelled in the Arts and Crafts style and repainted in cream. It opened onto the moor, and looked down towards Loch Tay and its array of boats.

At night, when she had finished educating the Molteno offspring, Madeleine would read to my mother. Their favourite books were full of maps and boats and adventure. They had enticing dust jackets plastered with line drawings like labels on a traveller's trunk. Arthur Ransome's tales of children and sailing and expeditions all took place far away from the confines imposed by grown-ups. The first, *Swallows and Amazons,* had been published in 1930. This was the book in which the Walker family's distant father gave them permission to sail and camp on Wild Cat Island with the immortal telegram: BETTER DROWNED THAN DUFFERS IF NOT DUFFERS WON'T DROWN. By 1939, there were seven books more in the Ransome series, and four still to come. Peggy-Ann devoured them. Just before she went to sleep, in that end-of-the-day quiet time between mother and daughter, perhaps an idea was born.

★

My mother as a child, looking very pleased with herself.

Designing the Chrysanthemum collection is a bit of a gamble. I have a few pages of drawings in my sketchbook but, as usual, no idea whether they will actually work, and neither time in hand nor a backup plan to come to the rescue in case they don't. All my eggs are in the one basket. Can I make a chrysanthemum flower to express the thoughts and emotions coming together inside me?

Physically, the three-dimensionality of this flower particularly intrigues me. I hope to capture the movement I've noticed, that twisting and turning of the outside petals. It's something I've observed in other picked flowers. Tulips often go a little wild after they've been cut, their petals bursting open and contorting out in all directions, in a kind of tarantella of the plant world.

At this point I remember a wonderful exhibition I'd seen at the National Gallery about fifteen years earlier, *Spanish Still Life (from Velázquez to Goya)*. By the time I reached Goya, dead creatures and lumps of meat were beginning to pile up like the corpses in his 'Disasters of War' series. Not what I was looking for. I still have the catalogue. On the cover is the show's poster painting: Cotán's severe arrangement of a hanging quince, a cabbage and a cut melon; simple, domestic and sharply lit against a black background. Inside I find the painting that struck me so much when I first saw it, a far lusher and more generous display of fruit and vegetables and cut flowers by a painter from Madrid called Antonio Ponce. He was later than Cotán, earlier than Goya, and less highly rated than either, but his work has an appealing extravagance about it.

12

In the *Still Life with Artichokes and a Talavera Vase of Flowers* you can hardly see the stone ledge on which the overflowing jug is balanced. Like my grandfather's potting-shed shelves, it's covered in stuff: untrimmed artichokes and apples and twigs and buds and foliage all jumbled up together. And just as I'd thought, the flowers themselves are just going over, doing that thing I was after. Rendered in brushwork that is strange and intriguingly super-real, the petals twist in chaotic beauty and lushness. Typically the background is dark and sombre, and the flowers, picked out in light, are positively luminous. Some look rather tired and old, still beautiful but heads drooping. Others are fresh and young and raring to go. There's a shining terracotta-coloured tulip in the centre that's as fresh as can be and just unfurling its petals. Far off to the right, a pretty white butterfly is fluttering out of view. It always catches me unawares and makes me wonder what is going on outside of the frame. There are no chrysanthemums in the vase but that doesn't matter. It's the spirit of the thing I'm after. I'll keep this page open as I do my designing to remind me.

Other paintings in another exhibition also come back to me. The riot of colour and movement produced by the 'phoenix of all flower painters', Jan van Huysum. Surely there were chrysanthemums in among those wildly outstretched tulips and bursting peonies? It doesn't matter; I don't need to check. The effect is what's so important. I'm going for ~~that~~ that off-centre craziness, whirling petals contorting in a dance, a sculptural, three-dimensional helter-skelter. And once I've made these little objects, I plan to put them together in a way that shouts glamour. I'm thinking Grace Kelly in the mid-fifties, driving along the coast road at Monaco in *To Catch a Thief*, wind in her hair, lusting after diamonds and diamond-thieves. I'm also thinking of her last film, *High Society*. Perhaps I'll even add a string of pearls.

I have a photograph of Grace Kelly, rather a polished Hollywood-studio type of an image. She's reclining in a strapless dress with a big blossom-branch of a corsage across her breast and up to her collar-bone. It's an image I also intend to keep in mind while I design the

13

collection. It's big and it's blousy but it's also quite dazzling and desirable. Just as unforgettable is that haunting photograph of her 'rising from the sea' by Howell Conant. Her wet hair is swept back, the water just below her bare neck and shoulders like a mirror of soft swirling golds and grey-greens. A tiny drip of water hangs from her earlobe. Her natural beauty looks straight through me. It's intimidating. But what a jewel of a picture.

Whether I can get all this into a single flower is a technical problem as much as anything else.

My next stop is my local florist, where I buy a few chrysanthemums which I promptly destroy. I'm pulling them apart to find out how they work. What does a flattened petal look like? I draw and I make notes, and after a day or so I have a plan. I'm going to cut out layers of leaves, from big to small, which I'll bend into shape, soldering the layers together and building up the form as I go. But I'm not sure how it will work out, so the only thing to do is to experiment.

I draw several versions of the layers of petals. Some look like a child's drawing of a daisy; some have only three or four petals. I scan these into the computer, zooming in and out until I have a whole variety of sizes, ranging from the dimensions of a 10p piece to a tiny sequin. My sheet of A4 paper is completely covered in little petalled star-shapes. I take a guess, choose a few I particularly like, cut them out and stick double-sided tape on them. I'm ready for the workshop.

I have a cine film of my parents' honeymoon in Devon. They're pootling about in a little clinker dinghy, my father looking very handsome at the helm, and my mother beautiful and rather coquettish, her arm draped over a picnic basket in the bow. She raises a camera, a Zeiss by the looks of it. Snap! and a cheeky laugh. I love the fifties glamour of it all. And I love the boats, all wooden of course, beautifully handmade and proudly painted in blues and reds. The colours on old cine films are great too, subtle but also much simpler: faded turquoise water, blue-grey sky and a varnished hull glowing gold. My mother is dressed in rust-coloured canvas slacks and a blue smock, her jet-black hair shortish and slightly tousled. My father wears high-waisted black trousers, a white shirt and a blue canvas sailing smock, open at the front, and always has a cigarette in hand. Carefree, young and beautiful: the world was just waiting for them.

Boats brought my parents together. My father, Stuart, had learned to sail in Salcombe, crewing for Peggy-Ann's brother Bill during his college days. The three of them would pop over to France in a hapless old lifeboat that had been converted to sail. Long weekends in Cherbourg in cable-knit sweaters and cropped jeans. Stuart spent far too much time mucking about on the water or playing pool with his friends, so he kept getting sent down. By the time he graduated, Peggy-Ann was already heading up an architectural practice in Cardiff, where she promptly employed him.

They married in the summer of 1956. They look carefree enough in the film, but perhaps they're giddy with relief. The day before the wedding, Peggy-Ann was struck down with polio, most likely picked up at her hen-night party at the Turkish Baths in Tiger Bay – her very first visit to the steam rooms. The ceremony was postponed while Peggy-Ann was held down in a hoop in the Isolation Hospital, where she endured lumbar punctures performed by an Amazonian matron. She still recalls the screams of a boy with meningitis. She got married in a wheelchair, only standing for the photographs. The harbour at Salcombe was a substitute for their original honeymoon plan, sailing round the Isle of Wight.

A year later though, they revived the idea of that south-coast cruise and chartered a vessel called *Blue Moon of Skye*. At night, by lamplight, they read. Just as Madeleine had read Arthur Ransome aloud to Peggy-Ann in the castle in Scotland, my mother in her turn introduced Stuart to the stories. Lying on his bunk, with waves gently rocking the boat, a lantern swinging in its gimbals, it was the perfect setting. One book, the seventh in the series, particularly captured Stuart's imagination. *We Didn't Mean To Go To Sea* takes the Walker family to a new spot,

Pin Mill, upstream from Felixstowe. In an unexpected fog, the children find themselves accidentally sailing to Holland after losing their anchor on a falling tide. For the first time, Ransome's charmingly naive line drawings are accompanied by real rather than fictionalised maps. Stuart read the stories and traced the lines of the east-coast estuaries with a finger. On one map, titled *Voyage of the* Goblin, *showing how she came and went back*, he found the rivers Orwell and Stour and the North Sea. Here was a good place to explore.

When a couple of jobs came up in an architectural practice in Ipswich, home to Arthur Ransome's boat the *Nancy Blackett*, the decision was made. A series of trains and buses later, Stuart and Peggy-Ann arrived in Ipswich and walked the seven miles along the southern shore of the river Orwell through Wherstead, along the Strand, past Woolverstone and then to Pin Mill. A pint of Tolly Cobbold in the Butt and Oyster and they fell in love all over again. This time with the Suffolk coast.

They got those jobs and moved. Boarding houses to begin with, then they rented a tiny house in Waldringfield where my oldest sister Debbie was born. Shopping trips were made in *Titmouse*, a 15-foot dinghy with a crude ruddy lugsail, named after Tom Dudgeon's boat in *Coot Club* and *The Big Six*. Debbie would be wedged into the bow, first mate and shopping took the centre thwart and the skipper was at the helm. Three children on, they had moved to Groom House in Woodbridge. Once the Horse and Groom, a long white stripe on the façade disguised its name, but the smell of beer never left the place. It still wasn't quite right. They needed more space.

It's like putting on a favourite pair of slippers for me, coming into my workshop. Tucked away upstairs in a Victorian mews that has always been a working yard for South London artisans. Cobbles and blackened London Stock, with huge peeling rust-coloured doors, which would slide right open if they actually worked. Inside, the workshop is as big as a good-sized sitting room. Plenty of light, dusty whitewashed brick walls, not a square inch unused and everywhere stacked up with extremely useful bits and bobs. The main workbench runs down the wall opposite you when you enter, with places for three jewellers. I sit on the far left, nearest the window. The workshop also has a forge, a polisher, a sink, various tables and hundreds of drawers. It smells familiar, like home. The acoustics make you feel at home too, somewhere you've been for ever and spent a lifetime carefully filling up. Soft and comfortable and just right.

A jeweller's bench is typically set about a metre high and made from thick planks of a hard wood, perhaps 5cm thick. My old bench is MDF. I couldn't afford the real thing when I made it. At each workstation a semi-circle of about 60cm diameter is cut out, a block of wood that traditionally became the seat of a low three-legged stool for the jeweller to sit on. We prefer squishy modern adjustable office chairs these days. Under the cut-out is the skin: a piece of leather slung on hooks to collect the lemel, offcuts and filings of precious metal which can be recycled or sold back to the bullion dealer. At the apex of the cut-out is the jeweller's pin, a wedge-shaped piece of wood about the size of a pack of cards against which metal can be held and filed or cut or emeried or whatever. Each pin gets worn down into a different shape depending on how the jeweller works. It's a bit like a fountain pen, perhaps. I get rather protective if anyone borrows my bench.

To the left of the pin is my cutting-V. A rectangle of plywood with a V cut out of it, pivoted at one end so it can rotate out over the skin and I can hold sheet metal on it and cut into it. (I say *cut*, but the jewellers' term is to *pierce*.) In between each workstation is a hefty vice and, although the area around each cut-out is clear, the rest of the bench is piled up with all sorts of tools and machines. My chair is quite low, so the bench comes up to the height of my chest. As I sit at my bench with my arms by my side, if I bend my right forearm 90 degrees it is about 10cm below my cutting-V. The perfect position for piercing out.

It's time to tackle the chrysanthemum in earnest. I decide to cut out from a sheet of 0.6mm-thick silver. Rummaging in my scrap

① Sort out samples + make "other halves". . (Vio?)

② Make other sketches in book.

③ H.P. Work . Smaller Rose
              Smaller Lily.
              Rosary necklaces (to Emma)*

④ Bayeaux.

Life
Size?

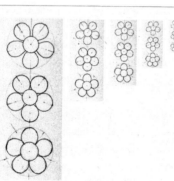

Feverfew / Daisy   Campion   flower   Chrysanth

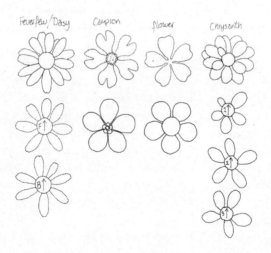

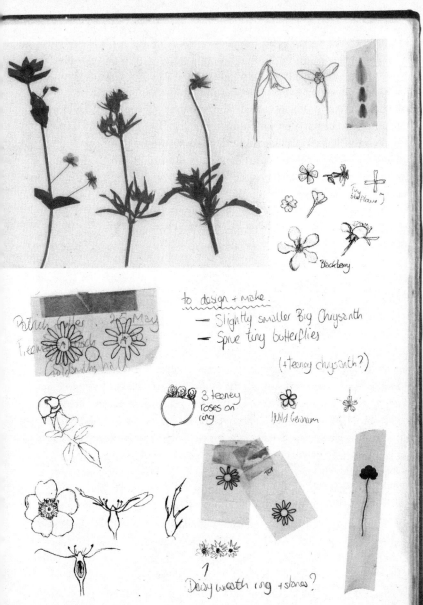

Blackberry.

to design + make.
— Slightly smaller Big Chrysanth
— Spire tiny butterflies

(+teeny chrysanth?)

Patrick Miller ... 25 May
Treona ...
Coldsmiths Hall

3 teeney
roses on
ring

Wild Geranium

Daisy wreath ring + stones?

box, I find an offcut the size of a standard Post-it note. I use double-sided Sellotape to stick my printed petal shapes onto the silver, as close as possible to each other, so as not to waste too much metal.

I have four or five piercing saws, but my favourite isn't the best. It's still the very first one I bought before starting college, and I've been cutting with this saw for almost thirty years. Burnished brown steel and wood, it has its peculiarities but I hardly notice them any more. For very fine thin sheet work I'll use a really thin blade, as thin as a hair: a 6.0, toothed along one side. You want the teeth to face downwards so the saw cuts on the pull, so I draw the saw blade across the sleeve of my T-shirt to feel for the direction of its teeth before fastening it into the C-shaped saw frame. Top first, a wing nut secures one end. Then, handle to chest, braced against the bench, I press into my ribs to tension the frame, and fasten the other end of the saw blade. With the release of pressure it draws tight like a bow. Ping . . . a sweet high note and it's perfect. My left hand firmly clamps the silver sheet onto the cutting pin and I start to cut.

My eyes hurt. It always takes a while to home in. It takes time to focus on details so tiny and necessarily so close. The job is 6 inches from my eyes and I hold the saw frame precisely upright. I saw using the full length of the blade, long strokes, the saw doing all the work, while my eyes stay directly above the cut. Each time I raise the saw it just brushes my cheek. My back is as rigid and upright as the saw blade. The rhythm of the taut moving blade is only interrupted when I pause to brush away the silver dust, which accumulates and conceals my drawing.

I cut out each layer of petals. Each layer has about twelve petals, and there are seven layers, the outside being the largest, going right down to tiny petals which will form the tight ball in the centre of the flower. Then I work on the texture of each petal. The effect needs to be linear and organic. It's slow and laborious work. There are technical words for this. Chasing and repoussé make the most of the malleability of metal, stretching and manipulating it from either side. Laying the petals on a leather pad and holding a punch in my left hand, I hammer with my right.

The harder I tap, the more the petals curve up to take the shape of the punch. The outside petals twist wildly in various directions, but as I work on the inside petals they become more even. Each layer is then soldered together in the right sequence, the central petals forming a tight ball. It starts to take shape, almost what I'd wanted, but still there is something wrong, something alien about this ball of tortured silver. It's like an insect from another world. Not gorgeous, but unsettling. Where's the glamour in it? Where's the brash charm? It's hard to put my finger on what is wrong. But I realise this whole idea of the twisting petals just isn't working.

I asked my mother recently why they chose such a vast, impractical house when they had no money and little chance of making any. She said it was because it had three staircases and she thought it would be great fun for us kids. Actually it had four.

They found The Old Parsonage off the main road in Woolverstone, an odd strung-out kind of village, with a school and a post office but no pub. The house was falling apart. It was the biggest in the village, with the exception of Woolverstone Hall, which at that point was a London County Council boarding school. The gardens of The Old Parsonage led down towards the river Orwell, and it was a short sail from there to Pin Mill.

As well as the many staircases, it had umpteen rooms. Along the eastern side they all interconnected on the first floor through a series of little antechambers, so a small boy could hide almost anywhere. There were attics, cavernous cellars, drawing, sitting, and dining rooms, halls, a school, a forge, stables, garages and I don't know what else. Ever since the departure of the parson at the turn of the century, the house had been left to crumble, bit by bit. By the time my parents arrived, the gardens were far from spectacular, the tennis courts were used as goose pens, greenhouses had sagged and cracked and the orchards were long-legged and overgrown.

Suffolk was, in those days, very much off the beaten track. On the way to nowhere, it was still untouched by the rest of the world –

just the place to escape the prejudices of 1950s Britain. Aldeburgh and Snape had become a bohemian retreat for an artsy crowd. Benjamin Britten and Peter Pears tucked themselves away there, and it certainly never occurred to me that there was anything unusual about the eccentric same-sex couples who used to come to tea with us. Why shouldn't a woman wear men's clothes and smoke with a cigarette holder? I've often wondered whether these unconventional, creative individuals were drawn to the area because of the remarkable lack of a middle class. There was nobody to pry or to gossip, and certainly no one to judge. The toffs were all completely crackers and sleeping with their sisters, while the common people were no bother – far too busy working and besides, it wasn't their place.

The house was bought, but it had to be made habitable. Stuart worked his days in the office and spent every spare minute fixing up the old place. In 1964 The Old Parsonage was ready enough for the family to move in, two parents and four kids by this time. (Four years later one more, Tom, would arrive.)

I have an image of us with our decrepit 1926 Humber parked at the end of the long drive, piled high with luggage and looking like Chitty Chitty Bang Bang without the shiny bits. You couldn't have called it a convertible because it didn't convert. It simply had no roof and when it rained we all got wet. Just as well for the dilapidated garages you see behind, which would once have housed several grand carriages. Enormous black doors and small windows all milked up with cobwebs. To the left is the old forge and stables, with a hayloft above.

Me, fast asleep on a pile of sand at The Old Parsonage, circa 1964.

A high wall joins the stables to the main house and there is a gateway in it, which leads into the walled gardens.

A big pile of sand is heaped on the drive and the sun is shining. The smallest of the children has toddled off to investigate. Finding the warm sand soporific, he lies down and falls asleep. His eldest sister, Debbie, is keeping an eye on him while Peggy-Ann and Stuart begin to unpack. Nikki is helping. (She's always helping, always looking after the little ones.) Her hair is as black as her mother's, cut short like a boy's. Where's Roddy? Even at three he was a right little

My father at the wheel of our clapped-out 1926 Humber on the drive at The Old Parsonage. This photo was taken by my mother in 1964.

bruiser, with big red cheeks. He's probably off looking for spiders to eat. I'm the sleeping baby, watched over by my sister. Neglected or protected, I look extremely content.

This was the start of a childhood spent between woods and river in the wilds of Suffolk. Grown-ups I remember only in glimpses and glances. There were always lots of people in the house and lolling around in the walled garden, swooping me up and whisking me off. Plonking me down in the long grass while I was still small enough. I look back on this period of my life with a mixture of fondness and disbelief, piecing together the details through a thick warm blanket of honey-coloured haze. Danger lurked in the shadows, but we grew up as free as birds, at liberty to explore and experiment as we liked. Perhaps the occasional relative or nanny issued orders or instructions from time to time – somebody must have told us what to do, once in a while, surely? Perhaps not. Certainly my parents seemed blissfully unconcerned about their offspring. Other than their occasional inadvertent attempts at filicide, I remember them having little to do with us. Left to our own devices, we hunted and we fought, we fished and we camped. And I drew and I made things.

I'm cutting out another set of petals. This chrysanthemum will have fewer petals on each layer and each will be a little fatter. Once again it comes out harsher than I'd planned, so I go back into my design studio and redraw the original petals, making them deliberately softer and fatter, with fewer in each layer. Third time lucky, it's just right. When I show it around the studio, people smile warmly, and relief makes me extravagant. I know what I'm doing now, so I make about ten more flowers, in varying shapes and sizes, and I make buds and leaves too and turn the petals into little settings for pearls and it all starts falling into place.

When I've got several convincing blooms and a fine selection of foliage, I send the originals off to be cast. That way I'll have a number of pieces to play around with. It's like casting a bronze statue, but in miniature – the lost-wax method. After making a rubber mould from the original, my casters inject wax into it to create an almost exact replica, which can then be encased in plaster. When the plaster, now set, is heated in an oven, the wax melts away, leaving a cavity into which molten silver can be injected. Break open the plaster, and hey presto . . . the casting, a near-exact replica of your original piece. Of course it's never perfect and there is often quite a bit of work to be done on a casting to bring out the fine details or textures, but originals can be reproduced faithfully. If I'm lucky, I'll get the castings back in about a week or so. It can be a tense wait.

It's 2011, late autumn, and my father is dead. I'm standing in his workshop at my parents' house in Framlingham surrounded by his old tools, a wave of sadness washing over me. It's a mess. Unused for several months, it's become a dumping ground for anything without a home: broken garden furniture, boxes of rubbish, old vacuum cleaners. I'm not ready to sort out any of his tools, but I want to make a start at clearing out some of the crap. Make some space, ready for when we divvy up and share out what remains of a lifetime of making things. The workbench he built while he was at school stands against the wall on my left. It has a shelf and a tool rack, and all the chisels and screwdrivers are still in their proper holes, arranged from narrow to broad. Old tools with handles polished smooth from a lifetime of use, the steel a warm brown colour, brass collars and studs bright and shining in the half-light, just exactly as they were in his workshop at The Old Parsonage. I spot his leather-bound tape measure; its brass winding crank folds back into the case with a satisfying snap when you're done. *Measure twice and you'll only have to cut once,* he would patiently explain. It pains me to see some other tools lying on the shelf, with no holes cut to house them. Tools we took from *his* father's workshop on the day of *his* funeral. Just as old and just as cared for. Two generations of tools.

I take a few minutes to soak it in and look around. I spot an old plane, which I first learned to use when I was about six. That brace-and-bit drill, steel and wood, with huge bits whose names I love: auger bits (little screw tip and long spiral fluting); centre bits (my favourite – their screw tips pull the cutting edges onto the wood, slicing their way through). This centre bit here even sounds good as it cuts. In fact, it smells good too. I think about cutting a hole in fresh green oak, or drilling into a slow-grown hunk of larch or deal. Every sense engaged. Somewhere in this workshop I'm sure there is even a gimlet bit. Too old-fashioned even for my father, it's a stubby little thing for which I still have an affection. I used to use a gimlet to cut the holes for the steering on our go-carts.

Best make a start. I empty out boxes and boxes of stuff for the dump. Old plumbing equipment, offcuts of plastic pipe, broken toasters and fan heaters, and masses of discarded bits of wood. I make a pile for chucking and a pile to give to nieces and nephews. And then at the back I find a pretty red-brown oak box, polished, and about the size of a large, wide shoebox. It's beautifully inlaid with ebony and little mother-of-pearl discs. The lid slopes at an angle. It's a writing box, I realise. I hesitate before opening it. By definition, it must be private. Who does it belong to and why is it here now?

It's not locked. The box is full of letters, mostly addressed to my grandmother Madeleine. Dodo, we used to call her, for she always seemed too sharp and intelligent and remote to be addressed as 'granny'. I liked her very much, though we only saw her about once a year, at Christmas. She always had a hint of glamour about her.

Lots of these letters are from Dodo's children, at different stages of their lives, but some are much older, written in her own childish hand to her grandparents or her aunt when she was away at school. The light is failing and I have a train to catch so I'll have to take these with me and come back soon to finish emptying the workshop.

I take the 19.30 from Wickham Market and, in the dusk, we chug along the single-track line towards Ipswich, where I have to change. The train from Ipswich is very tatty but not too busy. I find a seat with a table, put the old writing box on the seat beside me and take out all the letters. I'm still in a sorting mood and I feel I should organise them: letters to return to my uncle Bill in one pile, those for my mother in another. Older letters and various certificates I put in a third pile. Inside the writing box there is also a little compartment for storing pens. This is empty but almost subconsciously I fiddle with it, just in case I've missed something. The bottom of the penholder seems much higher than the bottom of the box. It occurs to me that there must be a space beneath it. I push down firmly on

26

one end and suddenly the other end opens, revealing a secret compartment. Inside, there is another small bundle of letters.

Looking up from my shabby seat on this rickety old train rattling its way to Liverpool Street, excitement rises in me. *This like a film*, I think. Across the aisle, a bored-looking young mother is concentrating on ignoring her sweet-eating children. She's absorbed in a gossipy magazine. An elderly couple doze two seats down. It almost seems odd that they've noticed nothing.

At first glance the letters from the secret compartment look similar to the others, the odd certificate or a letter to an aunt, but one – in an unusual hand – catches my eye. It is addressed to Madeleine, sent from Oxford and written on yellowing, rather crumpled paper (I imagine my grandmother reading and rereading it) squared, in that continental style. It opens with the words: *My dear, dear darling.* Of course, I turn immediately to the signature, but there's no name to be read. It's just an intimate squiggle, barely even an initial. You would only sign your name like that to someone who knew you very well. I return to the beginning and scan through three pages of heart-broken passion, the final pleas of a spurned lover. *Oh, could I speak English,* he writes, *oh could I touch your heart, you could not kick me away like a dog. And yet I hope, I always hope.* He is all alone in Oxford now, sitting, sitting, his head buried in his hands. He recalls in broken sentences the joys of their former companionship, daily walks, discussions of poetry. But he's coming to London for a few days. They have one last chance at happiness, it seems. Couldn't she meet him at Paddington the following Monday – his train will arrive at 4.20 p.m. – and they could go to the British Museum, and she could read him the poems she talked of . . . ? *Will you come to Paddington Station and help me to find out an hotel? I arrive Paddington next Monday at 4.20 p.m. Dearest Madeleine, will you write to me that I see you again?*

It's the only love letter I find. Curiosity overwhelms me, and from the train, I phone my mother. She is disappointingly uninterested in the whole thing. She does remember something about a German boy.

Madeleine knew him before Charles, and thinks perhaps he was interned, or deported because of the war? Impossible. The chronology is out. This letter is dated 11 October 1929, surely too early for anti-German feelings in Britain, so long after one war and well before the outbreak of the next? I check through the papers in my third pile and find Madeleine's wedding certificate. She married Charles on 9 August 1930. I wonder what happened to our passionate German? For a moment, I'm confused. The dates don't seem to be adding up. I even manage to convince myself that Madeleine must have been well and truly pregnant when she married Charles.

In the harsh artificial light, I look up from my table strewn with old letters and catch my own reflection in the dark window. The dull mundanity of the tatty old Ipswich train to Liverpool Street is reflected behind me, and all at once my curiosity is overtaken by a sense that I'm prying into real lives, lived by real people. I feel terribly guilty, so I pack all the letters up in the old writing box. They've stayed there ever since. But that little story I'd started telling myself about the blousy chrysanthemum flower, a story in silver and gold, is beginning to change. It's taking on a life of its own.

While I wait for the castings to come back, I have another thought. I love working with other people and have recently employed a young Norwegian graduate from Central St Martins whose eye for the 'now' has impressed me. Ulrikke Vogt is just the person to shake things up a bit and freshen my designs. She's imaginative about construction and there's glamour in her clean Scandinavian style. So together we do a few sketches.

Remembering the Hollywood photograph of Grace Kelly with the corsage, we draw the jewellery on the body instead of floating on a page. I even buy a mannequin so we can see how things sit. By the time the castings come back we're ready to begin the job of constructing each piece, playing with the forms and experimenting with different chains and stones. Over the course of the next week the collection starts to take shape. At this point the other young women in the workshop become involved too, and I begin to take more of a back seat. My job now is to keep the collection on track and channel everyone else's enthusiasm.

By the end of week two I can stand back and look at the pieces with detachment. I'm happy. Perhaps not everything is in there. Maybe there's some elusive aspect of the flower I haven't quite fully expressed this time. But I've got my sketchbooks. It doesn't have to end here. And my relationship with the chrysanthemum has developed along the way, obscurely and unexpectedly. I have a real connection to this flower now.

The new collection has allure and panache and it makes me smile. I'm ready to put it on show, and see if the world agrees.

The Bee

The purest moment of creation is right at the very start: that tiny inkling, the appearance of the spark of an idea. It's got to have enough about it to keep you at the bench, grinding away, hour upon hour and day after day. And it doesn't stop there. It has to grow into a full collection. A beautiful simple centrepiece that anyone can wear. Several of these, in fact. And then some other stars, much more lavish, that will photograph well. Not to mention a supporting cast, earrings and necklaces, rings and bracelets. That first idea needs to be able to maintain your excitement for the next few years, as it grows from a fleeting thought inside your head into something that a stranger can walk away with from a boutique in Tokyo or Saint-Germain, and treasure for the rest of her life.

One of those moments came to me once in Switzerland, when I was climbing up through the forests of Grindelwald, retracing the path taken by Sherlock Holmes on his way to his final, fateful meeting with Moriarty at the Reichenbach Falls. As Watson did Holmes, my companion had briefly abandoned me, and I was enjoying the solitude. Eventually I sat and rested, settling on a cool rock. The lower branches of these tall pines were bare. Thin shafts of light pierced the scented canopy and fell on puddles of rainwater collected in the rocks and mosses. It smelled of damp woody earth, and pine, and promises of a summer to come. Delicate flowers grew in the crevices – dog's-tooth violets and mountain pasqueflower, with downy purple heads drooping like bells. Others, tiny ones, I didn't recognise. A scattering of mushrooms had popped out from the lush brown peaty soil, fleshy caps on spindly stalks, looking as if they hadn't been there a few minutes earlier. As I sat and watched, a couple of ants went about their business. I tracked their path from where I sat. They were purposeful, and oblivious to me. A few bees flew low. It was early summer so I guessed they were looking for a good place to nest. You could almost see them deciding, bumbling around over crevices and rotten tree trunks, checking out one spot after another. One was distracted by an encounter with a violet with curled-back petals and irresistibly laden stamen. I could see the bee suspended, hanging on, legs powdery with pollen.

This is exactly it, I thought. This has got it. It wasn't so much the scene itself, but the moment, which had an element of fantasy and magic about it, exactly what I wanted to explore in the new collection. Dark and light. a kind of fairy tale. But it was also very real. I breathed it in, felt it on my skin. I was part of it, and I wanted to tell the world about it.

These days I recognise those glimpses of an idea more easily, although this part of the making process has evolved in me quite gradually. The compulsion to turn a *feeling* into an object. When I was much younger, the sensation of making was exactly the same, but there was no thought of exploring an emotion, or at least I was never aware of it. Not the childish me. Then it was all about function: wars to be won, cash to be made.

And my designs simply emerged from whatever materials I could lay my hands on. Scraps nicked from building sites. Debris from the marina. Bartered treasures from the binmen. There were rich pickings if you knew where to look. And there was always a high point in my scavenging year: the village fête, held in our gardens, which marked the start of the long summer holidays.

A wonderfully festive mood swept through The Old Parsonage during the build-up to the fête. The weather hadn't been great so far that summer of 1972, but it didn't matter very much to us children. Both house and gardens swarmed with people, all busy with preparations of one sort or another. Except Roddy and me. We were lying low, flat on our stomachs in the hayloft above the old stables, hiding from the grown-ups and keeping a good eye on proceedings. You never knew when there might be a chance to slip out and take a toffee apple or sneak away some sweets.

We called this place the Barn, and it made a perfect lookout. It was dark and smelled of musty rotten wood and hay. The Barn hadn't been used for decades and everything was just as it had been left, quietly decaying. Old bits of horse tackle, the odd pitchfork and a few rusting chains still hung on the red-brick walls. The floor was so rotten that grown-ups couldn't visit. Here and there, rough pieces of wood patched holes where heavier children had fallen through. One narrow window overlooked the drive, the other faced the back gardens and orchards. Most of the glass was smashed in both. Shafts of sunlight pierced the sagging pantile roof and I remember they looked almost solid to me. I used to try and grasp them, breaking and chopping them with my hand, examining tiny dancing dust particles, which shone like gold.

Today, as always, the signal for lunch was a loud bell. We leaped up, lowered the ladder through the trap door, and hurried to the house. Lunch was a help-yourself affair in a crowded kitchen. There were jugs of beer on the dresser, and elderflower cordial. Debbie and Nikki were in charge, handing plates to neighbours and wrapping knives and forks in squares of kitchen roll. They wore their hair long now, parted in the middle. This was the era of tight-fitting striped tank tops over loose white blouses with the top buttons fastened. The girls' high-waisted purple cords swished efficiently as they moved. We boys, in checked shirts and T-bar sandals, managed to shove our way to the table, where a couple of loaves of white bread sat on a blue-and-white gingham cloth. A bowl of tomatoes from the garden sat alongside cheese, preserves and some hard-boiled eggs. Roddy and I spooned runny strawberry jam onto badly cut chunks of bread and butter and ducked outside to sit and eat on the trunk of a fallen tree, where we were soon joined by the girls and a jam-smeared Tom.

The walled garden was as full as we'd ever seen it. Against the back wall, opposite the house, a coconut shy was half built. No coconuts yet. Trestle tables lined the other walls, waiting for their games. The grown-ups sat on two long benches either side of another wooden table, which bowed in the middle like a hammock. Mugs of beer with cheese and pickle in the sun. Next to the fallen tree was its stump, cut off at about waist height. The top surface was spiked with twenty or so 6-inch nails, waiting for the how–hard–can–you–whack–a-nail competition to begin. Someone had left a hammer on the log in readiness, and Roddy picked it up experimentally, felt its weight, eyed the nails. There was a yell from the house. Roddy scowled, dropped the hammer, and flicked a few bees off his bread and jam. Pesky buggers.

The girls, defeated by the bees, scooped up Tom and retreated into the safety of indoors. Roddy and I followed along the tree trunk, a jump over the herb bed (grabbing a sorrel leaf on the way) and in through the scullery door. An armful of flowers lay by the old butler's sink waiting to be put into vases; a box of apples, ready to be dipped into molten toffee, had been left next to the wellington boots on the flag-tiled floor. Debbie pulled the larder door shut as she passed, glancing in at shelves packed with jars of preserved fruits and jams. In the kitchen the girls settled Tom with his crusts up on a stool at the table and got back to their jobs: lunch to clear, cakes to bake, more cordial to bottle. I scooped up some sugar in my fingers and poured it into my mouth, and then we darted through into the living room, which was still strewn with half-sewn bunting. Prizes for the lucky dip were piled on the floor next to rolls of old wallpaper, ready to wrap them.

We crept out through another door, along a dark corridor and into the workshop by the back stairs. The beat-the-buzzer contraption sat silent on the bench: lunch had interrupted Stuart's repairs.

Through the workshop and into the schoolroom, full of jumble. And outside again, where a large sack with a target painted on its front gaped half-stuffed, a bale of straw beside it. The archery competition was only slightly less exciting than the plate-smashing. But they were nothing compared with the climax of the Woolverstone summer fête.

Hey, listen! It's here. Quick.

A tatty blue van was parking under the yew tree. Peggy-Ann had beaten us to it, so it was back to the Barn for cover. Through the glassless window we watched: four burly men got out and opened the back doors of the vehicle. Our eyes widened. We grinned at each other.

Oh, well done, chaps! You couldn't possibly just carry it up to the Top Field for me? Peggy-Ann spoke in the uncommanding voice of one who had no need to issue orders. Her will was always done. She turned, and perhaps the silk scarf knotted at her neck caught the breeze jauntily.

The men's grunts and wheezes could be heard from the Barn as they struggled to unload the old piano from their van. Off they staggered, past the old stables and coach house, with a passing glimpse through a wrought-iron gate at the beer drinkers. Roddy and I scampered down the loft ladder and followed at a safe distance. Around the wall where almond trees grew in pretty curved bays, along a narrow path through the kitchen gardens, with their awkward stacks of terracotta flowerpots, and then past the crumbling hothouse.

Regular halts were called for, with much brow-wiping and breath-gathering, and a few furtive scowls at Peggy-Ann. Her smile was as unshakable as her directions about exactly where to step and how to stand and when to heave and mind the precious plants. There were a lot of these. In stops and starts, the procession turned left at the tall ash with its Tarzan rope and views up to the jungle. And still we followed, just out of sight.

At Top Field at last. The tennis courts had long ago been given over to ducks and geese. The blackened bonfire site was in this field, and from here another path led past a giant walnut tree, through into orchards full of ancient apple trees. But the piano need not go so far: after some final huffing and heaving, it's in position at last, just by the walnut tree. And Peggy-Ann has decided it's safe to leave the men. First though, she voiced a final thought.

While you're at it, there's another piano in the hall. Would you be angels? Debbie will show you the way.

You can't have a piano-smashing competition with just one piano.

When I thought about it later in life, it seemed a barbaric sport, not far off book-burning. But now that I've done a little research about why we were destroying pianos with such glee each summer in Suffolk, it makes more sense to me. These were the early days of affordable imports from the Far East. Desperate old instruments, which had expanded and contracted in the dampness of drafty village halls, instruments that tortured brave performers and turned beautiful melodies into honky-tonk tunes were being joyously cast aside and replaced by wonderful new pianos. Music lovers rejoiced! But music was liberated at a price: the abandonment and disposal of hundreds of these old faithfuls. I imagine that for the grown-ups, it was more a celebration of the end to disharmony than a delight in the destruction of art. For Roddy and me, it was simply a means to an end.

Two beautiful upright pianos now stood beside the walnut tree in Top Field. One dark, one lighter. One was the stranger from the village, the other familiar from The Old Parsonage's own hall. And now we were alone with them. I gently ran my fingers over the smooth surfaces. The shiny lacquered wood had an intricate inlay, cut in symmetrical patterns of leaves and ribbons. The grain on the veneer glowed in the sunlight with the depth and lustre of a tiger's eye. I lifted the fall to reveal the black-and-white keyboard beneath and my fingers began to move across it. Outside, the notes sounded odd and very out of tune. We pressed the foot-pedals hard and listened to the strange noises that resounded round the field. We raised the hinged lids. So much material. Wood and strung steel wires. Brass and ivory. Ebony too, of course. But best of all, hidden under the back of the keys, right inside the heart of each old piano, we knew we would find lead.

By mid-morning the next day the fête was in full swing and all the village children were jollying along, eating cakes and shattering crockery and bashing nails. There was no lunch to speak of. At teatime, an announcement was made and everyone bustled up to the Top Field. Two teams of four brawny fellows were there already, facing their pianos, a sledgehammer in each hand. It was time for the finale. The first team to reduce their piano to matchsticks was the winner and this was a serious business. Chelmondiston and Tattingstone might have had five or more instruments at their fêtes, but here in Woolverstone we really knew how to smash a piano at speed. Was Peggy-Ann's friend Jimmy there, Britten's favourite percussionist? Quite likely. Other musicians certainly were.

On your marks . . . Ready your hammers . . . and with the shrill blow of a whistle, the first blow smashed down onto a piano. A frenzy of walloping ensued. Into all that delicate marquetry and varnish, the men – terrifyingly powerful – crashed their rough steel. Grunts and shouts were heard, smashes, twangs and notes! Notes as the pianos played an awful death dance. Splinters of wood and ivory ricocheted off into the crowd. How long did it take? Time seemed suspended, but it was probably no more than a couple of minutes.

As quickly as it had started, one team let out a roar and a cheer and threw their arms in the air. Everyone clapped and called to one another. A second judge was needed to adjudicate. Beer was poured and backs were slapped. The competition was over. They had a winner: the team of farm workers from Mayhew's. And those beautiful pianos were gone.

But as attention turned to the wine and beer being served to the crowd, two small boys crawled among the debris. We were looking for what we could salvage: anything that could be sold for cash or

36

refashioned into something else, something far more dangerous than a piano.

On all fours, we sifted through the wreckage and sorted out useful from scrap. First in order of importance were the key leads: the small heavy cylinders of lead found in the backs of piano keys which give them weight and counterbalance. We sorted out piles of keys, black and white, to dismantle later. A few strings might be useful too, and of course any handy lengths of wood that were still unbroken. And there were always a few other interesting bits and bobs worth saving, bound to come in useful at some point. Roddy carried an armful of keys down to the stables while I fetched a screwdriver from the workshop to unscrew and salvage any catches and hinges. The afternoon drew on and the shadow of the tall ash lengthened over Top Field.

And then the grown-ups chucked the splintered scraps of beech and spruce onto the bonfire and set them alight, and long into the night they stood around warming themselves by the flickering light of two burning pianos. As for Roddy and me, we were well away with our spoils.

Back in the Barn now, we worked by the light of a candle. It was fiddly work, hatchets in hand at the chopping log, smashing each little lead weight out of its key and popping it into an old baked bean can. The oldest weights were white and encrusted with sugar of lead – salt of Saturn – and made our fingers taste sweet. Between bangs and chips and ringing metal sounds, we could hear the voices of grown-ups in Top Field. The house itself was eerily empty, every door open and all lights blazing, but not a soul about. Later, when I heard my sisters calling out for us at bedtime, we still didn't leave. Eventually we stole silently up the back stairs and into our beds. Tomorrow we would melt the lead and cast it. That was my speciality. And I couldn't wait.

Next morning Roddy and I headed out to our workshop while the house still slept. I found a catering-size tin can to fill with cold water and rummaged in a drawer for the tools we needed. Then we picked up our precious wooden moulds from the workbench. One piece of wood had a line of carved-out holes; the other a series of burned-out heptagons. If you heat a fifty-pence piece until it's red hot, you can burn an impression of it into soft pine or balsa wood. I discovered that if you're careful enough when you lift out the money, you're left with a perfect carbonised coin mould.

Even when empty, these wooden moulds were always given due honour. On this particular morning they were carried from the workshop to the Barn with the kind of gravity and care a tray of Sèvres china might demand. We collected our cans of lead nuggets from the night before and then it was back to Top Field, where the bonfire was still smouldering. Good.

Raking the hot ashes into a pile, we carefully built up the unburned pieces of wood from around the fire on top of the embers. Heads down, lips pursed for a good blow. Smoke gathered first, in a steady stream, and then the flame appeared. Soon the fire was good and hot again. On either side of the flames, we propped two bricks, balancing the first baked bean can between them. Then we looked around for more wood. (Not the last of the smashed-up piano keys, for these could not be wasted. There was nothing quite like their resilience for making crossbow triggers.) Roddy fed the fire while I watched and stirred the melt.

Starting at the bottom of the can, the lead nuggets began to collapse satisfyingly into their own molten pools. After fifteen minutes every last bit had melted into the next and the can was a quarter full of spinning silver liquid. There was a slight scum on top but this was easily skimmed off with an old spoon we'd brought up with us. Trial and error and plenty of burned fingers had nearly perfected the process. Then the Mole grips came out, pliers that locked securely onto the boiling can. I lifted the can slowly over the first wooden board. It felt incredibly heavy. That was always my job. I was the one who knew exactly how to pour, when to pour. I had an aptitude for the medium. Maybe I wasn't so good at running or fighting, but when it came to making things, I was a natural. As I carefully filled each cavity, I would blink and try to blow away the smoke that billowed up into my eyes. Then Roddy replaced the coin moulds with the second board and I filled up all twenty of the holes in that. And all from one can. We had lead to spare this time.

Ready? With our pocketknives we prised each counterfeit coin from the board and plopped it, hissing, into the cold water can. Ten little shining beauties. Then, using the tips of our blades, we got to work on the second board. Twenty gleaming pointed metal shapes: arrowheads for the crossbows and bullets for home-made blunderbusses. The arrowheads were perfect, the bullets all OK, but one or two of the coins would need some cleaning up if they were to work in the cigarette machine in town. We squatted smokily by the fire as the first rays of morning sun shone through the leaves of the old walnut tree. Eight weeks of holidays still to go.

Forging coins, or fashioning a prototype. The experimentation and creativity involved in overcoming technical difficulties still holds the same fascination for me today. Making a successful original means making a series of failures. The repeated frustration and disappointment is only made bearable by the belief that the end result will be worth it. When it does eventually go right and you can begin to see that tiny spark of an idea become real, an actual physical object appear which you have created from sweat, tears and sheer hard graft, it's another key moment. A flash of excitement is followed by a swift rush of doubt. Quickly . . . ask someone what they think. I dash off to show my colleagues. They're kind and they love it, of course – what else could they say?

But nowadays fifty-pence coins and harpoon heads no longer cut the mustard. Practical challenges are fun, but I need an emotional drive. A *feeling* to explore, ideas to express. Ideas that have a context.

This is how my bee is born. As it happens, at this particular time – it's 2007, a lingering summer – I'd just made a particularly delicate and pretty collection in silver with gold highlights. All very English countryside, teensy-weensy and self-consciously cute. So I want to move away from that mood and get a little bit saucy. A counterpoint. Something grown up. And that's when, among a great muddle of ideas whirring round in my head (picture an open filing cabinet with a fan trained on it at full blast) good old sex leaps to the fore. Sex is saucy, and so is lust. And I'd always felt I was better at the latter. But lust is a sin. I wonder why? Suddenly, I have a starting point.

I'm cross with myself because I've just missed a Lucas Cranach exhibition at Somerset House, but he's still on my mind. In fact he's probably what lodged this idea in my head. So I pull out all my old history of art books and do a bit of reading up. Forget about lust, I decide. Lucas Cranach is reminding me of the sauciest sin of all, the first and the best: original sin. Now I've got forbidden fruit to play with. *Adam and Eve*.

Cranach's apple is bang in the middle of his painting. The bite that's already been taken out of it is right in the middle of the apple, framed in passing by Adam's and Eve's delicate hands. The peel is just beginning to curl into the flesh: decay happens fast in Eden. Eve's fingers curl around the top as she offers the fruit to Adam. His hand accepts it more fastidiously. His finger and thumb hardly seem to grasp it. She's looking at him, just waiting. He's looking at the apple wistfully, soberly, sadly. Above their heads, the snake slithers down the tree towards Eve's head. But the creature could be looking straight out of the painting, at us.

Good old Adam and Eve. I'm not about to get theological about this. You can't call ideas of this kind thinking, not really. It's more of a train of thought. But one thing leads to another. Original sin is great because without it we would have nothing. No death, no toil, no sauciness either. And everyone would be walking round naked, which would be fairly unpleasant in real life. Without original sin nobody would have been begat, and nobody would have murdered each other and the whole world might have been quite dull. It's an odd sin because it had to happen. Temptation was always going to win. I like it because I can thoroughly identify with it — here's everything you could ever need, endless supplies of it all. Just don't touch that one little thing over there and you'll be fine . . . Of course, they were going to bite into the apple. It's human nature. And you can see in his face that Cranach's Adam knows it.

I like this painting a lot. The crispness of each detail: the subtle curve of Eve's big toe; the gentleness of the animals and the way each one seems to fix you with a forgiving gaze. But then I realise that I like Cranach's painting *Cupid Complaining to Venus* even more. Funnily enough, the pale crags and pine trees in the far distance remind me a little of Grindelwald. Here's another tree, more apples, another beautiful elongated nude with a branch twining suggestively through her bare legs. Venus's toe is remarkably similar to Eve's, and they stand in just the same way too, one straight leg slightly crossed in front of the other.

And there's poor little Cupid, hand on golden head just like Adam, quite baffled at what's happened. Bees are crawling all over his fleshy arm, bees on skin and feathery wings; huge bees, one with a head like a grinning skull and bizarrely, an extra pair of hairy legs. Cupid looks thoroughly fed up with them, as if he can't believe his bad luck. He hasn't even had the sense to drop their honeycomb yet. And I look at him and think, *You suck the honey, you pay the price.* Adam and Eve learned that one the hard way too. The inevitable pain of love.

Exhibitions and books and gardens and parks. I need information. This painting has belonged to London's National Gallery since the 1960s, so I can easily see it again. Much later I discover that it once formed part of Hitler's looted collection, and I'm glad I didn't know that before. At this stage I'm more preoccupied with natural history. What plants were there in the Garden of Eden? Figs, of course, and pomegranates. Ah well, artistic licence . . . let's put some passion flowers into the collection too, and a gorgeously textured snake, which means I can look forward to a trip to the zoo. And apples, and plenty of loving, and insects, and the bee. Don't forget the bee. The bee is the key, the sting in the tale.

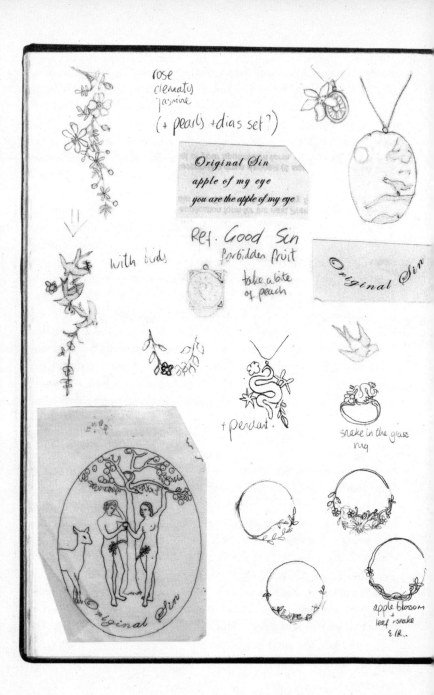

rose
clematis
jasmine
(+ pearls + dias set?)

Original Sin
apple of my eye
you are the apple of my eye

with birds

Ref. Good Sin
forbidden fruit
take a bite
of peach

Original Sin

+ pendant.

snake in the glass
ring

Original Sin

apple blossom
+ leaf + snake
E.R..

Original Sin - The Garden of Eden - Apple, Snake, fig leaf, Garden plants

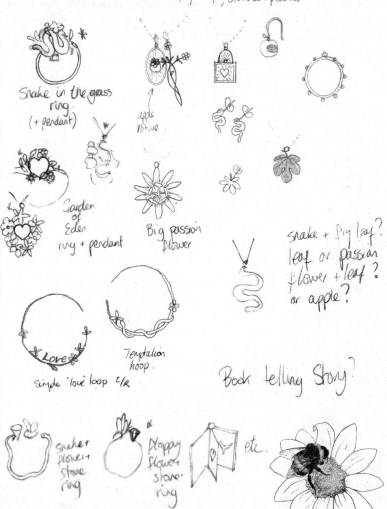

Snake in the grass ring (+ pendant)

apple votive

Garden of Eden ring + pendant

Big passion flower

snake + fig leaf?
leaf or passian flower + leaf?
or apple?

Love

Simple 'love loop' E/R

Temptation hoop.

Book telling Story?

snake + flower + stone ring

poppy flower stone ring

etc.

I find out more about Lucas Cranach, too. He had a sense of humour all right. You can see it in those poses. He was a friend of Martin Luther, a close friend, and he believed in his ideas. A good man. And he lived for ages. I find a portrait of him in old age – badger hair, white double-pointed beard, very plain, with just his own shadow in the background. He might have painted it himself; it could be by his son. He looks a kind man, and there's a softness about him you see in his work. I like him a lot. Looking again at his other paintings, I see respect and pathos. That's what I want too, for my bee.

More thinking and more research. I collect a million twigs and leaves and flowers. And I draw and I make notes and draw some more and I daydream. Finally it's time to start at the bench. There's only so much you can do on paper. I need to get into the workshop.

First things first: some serious procrastination. I tidy my bench, and in the process more distractions appear: something to repair or a half-finished project that demands attention. When the sum of the guilt of not getting started is equal to or larger than my ability to stall, I start the proper work. Apples and snakes and passion flowers all present their own challenges, but my plan is to focus first on one piece to tie the whole collection together. That centrepiece. The agony that comes with sweetness. The unavoidable sting. The bee.

Cranach is in my thoughts as I sit low at my bench. Searching through a small cardboard tray full of scraps of silver rod, I pull out a piece 15mm in diameter. It's about 10cm long so I can carve the bee from one end while holding the other. This is a piece that needs to have some weight. Physical weight, that is. But it's looking for presence too. Sorrow, regret, pathos. And also strength and femininity. Taking my piercing saw, I cut into the silver. I cut away the shape I'm imagining, first from above, and then from either side. Where my cuts seem wrong, I file away. The piece becomes too square, so I cut and file off the corners. Hours pass. My left hand hurts and I notice it's bleeding where I've been holding the sharp metal. I should have rounded off the 'handle' end of the job first.

Day One is a catastrophic failure. There's no point in persevering with this one. But I can't throw it away. I stand and stretch and take my bee to the office, where I pull a cigar box down from a shelf. A small junkyard of experiments and not-quite-right pieces. My eye scans its contents. Ha! That sputnik ring. I'll get that right some day. And a little box of melted nuggets. There are bugs and leaves and textured offcuts. I smile as I remember each disaster. It's like browsing through an old sketchbook, full of embarrassing mistakes with a few interesting experiments. Plop! I drop in the unfinished bee and snap the lid shut.

The weekend comes as a relief. An early morning cycle ride and a few hours on the allotment. The usual ferrying of children to and fro. Sunday is warm and I'm hoping to potter about in my shed with my bikes. But the kids run in with an emergency.

Hi there, girls, what've we got here?

A velvety bumblebee has got trapped in the house and exhausted itself. So they've put it in an open matchbox with some cotton wool and come for help. It must be on its last legs this late in the year, I think to myself. But three little girls are looking up at me, full of concern, and trusting me to know what to do.

Will it be OK, Dad?

Let's have a look now. A buff-tailed bumblebee, I think. Bombus *something . . . We'll look it up.*

And into the house we go to find my soft green copy of *The Observer Book of Common British Insects. Bombus terrestris, I discover. Ah, a female, of course, I say. She's bigger and prettier than a male. Do you see the sting in her tail? Look how smooth it is. Not like a honeybee's. No, she wouldn't die if she stung you, however many times. But she probably won't sting you either, if you keep on the right side of her. She's a gentle little thing.*

We put her in a bigger box, a cook's-size matchbox this time, with a little water. I suggest a snack for her so the kids rush off to pick a geranium flower or two. We fuss and try our best. The girls are a bit upset and I'm not at all sure how to fix poorly bees; I suspect we should let nature take its course and leave her be. But I go through the motions of tucking her up with a good selection of pollen-laden flowers and a drink in a comfy bed. We decide to let her alone, and find a sunny secluded spot in the garden to set her down.

Back with my bikes I keep thinking about her. She's our bee now. The kids really care for her and she's just what I've been looking for. She can be my muse and my model. I like the fact that she's a bit under the weather, that there's something a little sad about her. I go back to check on her, and find the kids still fussing over her box.

Leave her alone. She needs space and air to breathe.

And then I run back to the house for my camera and start photographing her, and I get my sketchbook and I take notes. The sitting only takes half an hour and I have all I need. I can't wait to get back to the studio.

It's not till after lunch on Monday that I can cut myself off from the outside world again. Surrounded by my notes and my pictures and my drawings, I start again on Day Two with a fretsaw whose blade is as thin as a hair. Again I begin to cut out the essential form from a thick silver rod. Filing away, holding the rough silver against my work-worn bench pin, I try to discover the shape inside, as if I can simply uncover something already hidden within the silver. It's a feeling you only get when you're carving. There are other techniques that give you a sense of something *growing* instead, but when you're cutting away at metal there's a real sense of revelation.

When I look up I notice it's dark outside. Where did the day go?

Back at my bench on Tuesday morning and there's my bee, just as I left her. But this morning my eyes are fresh. I pick her up. A little flash of doubt is followed by a skip of the heart. Then fear. But I'm pretty sure this is the one. So I sit down quickly, pull out a needle file and get straight back into it. The shape's all there, but there are some scruffy patches that need tidying up.

I pull on my dust mask and optivisors – the super-magnifying headgear that turns us all into hybrid insect species – and my surroundings retreat: the sound of the radio, the movements of other people filing and sawing or chatting about the jobs they're doing.

Me, working at the bench, in my Elephant and Castle workshop.

Mask and goggles shut me into my own little world and as I peer at my bee, we're on our own again. This is going to be just the job for my new tool, I decide. It's a setter's tool, bought it from Germany especially for something like this. It fits onto my micro-motor but instead of spinning, it taps, like a mini pile driver. It was designed for tapping over settings for stones, to keep them in place. But now I file it into a point and set it in motion with the foot pedal. Rat-tat-tat-tat like a ticker-tape machine. Working in small circles, I begin to texture the thorax. Each leg then has to be carved out separately and soldered on. Last of all the wings, tiny shapes traced from my sketchbook and cut out in wafer-thin silver. Each one is cautiously soldered in place, with care not to melt the solder of the previous joins. Then I engrave the fragile vein pattern into all four wings.

I sit back and look at her, and she looks wonderful. Just as I'd imagined. Everything I wanted to say, all my thoughts and emotions over the past months, finally encapsulated in this little piece of silver.

How could you not love her? She's soft and warm, she's very strong, and she'll sting you if you get in her way. But somehow she looks a little mournful as well, and there's something unreachable about her too. She could fly away any time.

The original bee taking shape on my workbench.

The closest I ever came to flying went down in family history as the Battle of the Barn. Flying, or falling?

A hot afternoon in the middle of August. We were lying in the cool darkness of the hayloft and doing very little. You could hear insects buzzing, and chickens scratching about below. In the distance a lazy-sounding lawnmower was chugging away. There were visitors of course; there were always visitors in summer. Their voices rose and fell as they chatted in the walled garden.

We were getting a little bored.

Out on the road, a car engine changed gear. It was coming this way. We heard the slamming of doors, and new voices. Another family had arrived and they joined the party in the walled garden.

All very nice.

A couple of children said please and thank you for their squash and biscuits and talked politely with the grown-ups. Roddy and I looked on from our hideaway. There was a shout from below, and some of our mates came shimmying up the ladder.

What's up, boys?

Would you take a look at this?

Mummy's boy, sucking up to the grown-ups.

We all peered down at the scene of tranquillity in the garden.

That's horrible, that is. We should get them with everything we've got.

We looked at each other and we made a pact. Death and destruction to the visitors.

With hardly a word, we began to fill buckets with water. Our weapon of choice was a bicycle pump and the technique was simple but it worked. You sucked up a load of water then screwed a piece of Lego into the end. A sharp shove on the pump and the Lego would shoot out at speed, stinging your target then soaking them with a jet of water. In case things got serious, several crossbows were loaded and ready to fire. Hundreds of apples were hauled up and I'd already prepared a huge pile of nut-and-bolt bombs. These took hours to make: a nut was partially screwed onto a bolt and a cap-gun cap pushed into the cavity. The rest of the space was filled with ground red match heads and another bolt screwed into the other end, good and tight. All the weapons were stacked by each window. We were ready for war.

Hold your fire, boys – the first shot is mine.

Roddy took aim at the smartest grown-up, who was standing over a woman who was lying on an orange sunlounger. He was definitely showing off.

A crack and a hiss. Direct hit. The Lego plug hit the man in the face and he yelped. Then came the water. His look of shock and confusion delighted us. The woman on the sunlounger screamed and spilled her tea.

From the house ran a formidable figure, furious and shouting. He was an old friend of Peggy-Ann and Stuart, and the screaming woman was his wife. Roddy and I really looked up to him. Now he was looking up at us.

You bloody stupid kids! That could have been someone's eye. Come down here at once for the bloody good thrashing you deserve.

As if. In the shadows of the Barn we didn't need to see each other's faces to know things were about to get serious.

Let 'em have it, lads. And we did.

There were four of us up there, all boys. We pelted and sprayed and chucked and shot and bombed. Most of the women and the

49

other children ran for cover but the men fought back as hard as they could. They threw back buckets of water and stones and apples. We kept hurling the bolt bombs, which exploded with a terrific bang as they hit the ground, sending each bolt bouncing off brickwork to fearsome effect. The men turned the hose on and fetched umbrellas. The boys reached for their crossbows. As the battle picked up pace, more people appeared from the house. But we had all the advantages of height and preparation.

Look out! They've got a ladder! I rushed towards the open window with a fresh handful of bolt bombs. Something hit me, or maybe I was pushed, or maybe I simply slipped.

I enjoyed the most wonderful floating sensation as I fell, that slow-motion feeling when seconds pass at a standstill. It was the first time I'd ever experienced it, and so it was quite the most marvellous. I landed on my head two storeys down on the cobbled floor of the old forge, and was knocked out cold. I'm told that I lay in a pool of blood while my sisters went to find a parent, and I woke to an odd metallic taste in my mouth and the smell of Dettol, which still always makes me think of sick. The parent had issued instructions to carry me up to bed and wrap a towel around my head to stop the bleeding. Some time later, perhaps the next day, Peggy-Ann visited me herself. She knew Nikki and Debbie were taking perfectly good care of me, because they always did, and injuries were par for the course at The Old Parsonage. There was no need to fuss. No duffer, so not dead.

Six months after my bee has flown the studio, Sophie Dahl is looking out from the cover of a glossy women's magazine. It's a closely cropped shot, just head and shoulders. Against the bottle-blonde of her hair and the black of her leather jacket and little polka-dot scarf, the colour that stands out is the bright shiny red of her perfectly outlined lips. This red lends an unexpected suspicion of green to her blue eyes.

The bee hangs at her throat. It's layered with another necklace, a pale stone on a very fine gold chain. Sophie's very pretty, but there is a strength behind her eyes. The bee wears well on her, for they have a lot in common. Looking back at her are Emma and me. Emma is my PR manager, we're in my studio, and I'm peering over her shoulder.

What do you think? she asks me.

The phone begins to ring.

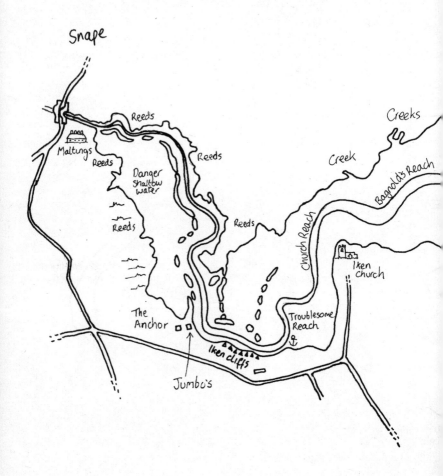

The river Alde from Snape Bridge to Aldeburgh

Snape

Maltings

Reeds
Reeds
Reeds
Reeds
Reeds
Reeds

Danger shallow water

Creeks
Creek
Bagnold's Reach
Church Reach

Iken church

The Anchor

Troublesome Reach

Iken cliffs

Jumbo's

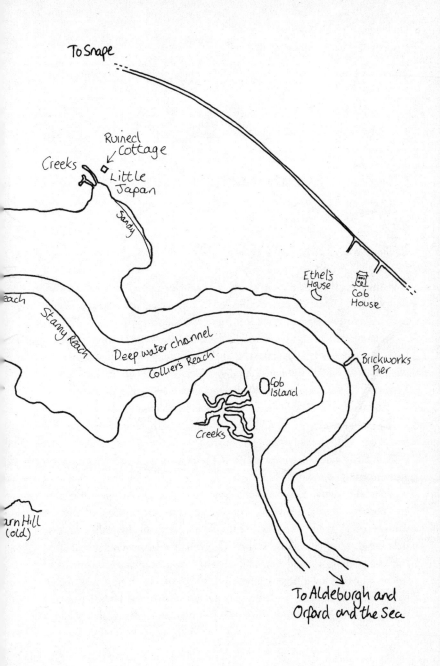

Two Turtle Doves

London, October 2010

I've had another one of my ideas. An idea which involves other people and which we will all come to regret, but which seems perfectly simple to me at the moment. I call a meeting.

How about a special Christmas collection? Like an Advent calendar but with twelve windows. We make just one piece for day one, two pieces for day two . . . you get it? Over twelve days. We'll call it 'The Twelve Days of Christmas Trunk Show'. The beauty of it is that every piece is an exclusive, but you don't know what's behind a window before it's open. So do you rush to buy one of the pieces on day three, or wait and see what's behind the day four door? It'll be really fun!

About fifteen faces look back at me with a mixture of confusion and fatigue.

We call events where we make a special selection of one-off exclusive pieces a 'trunk show'. It sounds odd now, but in the old days the dresses for a private sale would literally arrive from the fashion house in a trunk, and the name stuck. There was a time when we'd send out the invitations and I'd pack up a suitcase of jewellery to take to sell at an office or a film studio. Nowadays we do these trunk shows for special occasions, and tend to keep them local. It was the first time I'd thought of trying something similar on our website. My idea was to make twelve exclusive designs and release one of them each day for the first twelve days of December. Nobody would know what the next day's design might be, but we'd tempt customers with clues in the form of rhymes and illustrations.

I'm having trouble explaining the project clearly, but one thing about it is apparent: it's going to make lots of extra work for everybody, and they're already working far too many hours. I need to infect them with my own excitement.

And we'll tie it into the song, but add our own twist. Five gold rings obviously, and the pear – can't wait to do that . . . and I've had an idea for the second day, you know, the turtle doves . . .

I think everyone is resigned to the fact that there's no escape from this, so we're off.

It's late in October so there's no time to waste. First of all, there's the song to think about, 'The Twelve Days of Christmas'. I'd heard that every line of it symbolises something religious, though I'm a bit hazy about the details. Apparently it was a secret way to teach Catholic children their catechism during the years of oppression. The three French hens supposedly represent Faith, Hope and Charity. My thoughts wander as I do a little research. If I ever keep chickens again, that's what I'll call them, I decide, Faith, Hope and Charity, imagining my own French hens scratching around for worms. But before I've had a chance to speculate about the swans a-swimming, I discover that the religious interpretation turns out to be a twentieth-century fabrication, without a shred of evidence. But since my faith is in nature, I'm not too worried about that. It just gives me free rein and a bit more scope for reinvention.

I'm reminded of my own symbols of Christmas, images from my childhood. An impudent blue-tit pecking through the foil of our milk bottles on the doorstep, chickens racing towards an arc of grain as it lands in the snow, the whirr and wobble of a partridge in flight. I'm not going to change the second day, though. This is the piece I'm most looking forward to making: Two Turtle Doves. It's something I keep coming back to in different forms, over and over again.

And I know exactly why. There's a fleeting image from the past, which has never quite left me.

There's a brick bridge in Snape, crossing the river Alde where it narrows. Skinny and shivering, I stood there at dusk by my parents' car with my older brother. It wasn't raining, I don't think, but it was cold. My shorts were hand-me-downs from an older sister and I wore a rather itchy speckled brown jumper and a grey cotton anorak. On my feet were the faded blue sailing pumps that I loved because they were proper sailor's shoes.

We began to lower the old canvas canoe into the muddy water. The boat was gunship-grey. In fact, everything was beginning to look rather grey by this time: the cold Suffolk evening sky leached colour from the landscape. Grey to start with, like the canoe, the water and the mud are unchanged.

It'll be super, darling. What an adventure! You have the maps and look, here's a torch. (A flash of hope as my brother tested it.) *We'll be in Cob House waiting for you, of course. Just find the island and you'll find the house. Up the path from the jetty on the north shore. We'll keep some supper for you. Goodbye, goodbye!*

Even the red Ford Escort looked grey now. Only the headlights glowed yellow through the reeds, then swung away. The crunch of tyres on gravel drowned final farewells. We could just make out our younger brother squashed into the boot, while the older sisters waved from the back seat, sitting cosy. Then the car pulled over the little bridge and disappeared.

It was hardly the first time our mother had forced us into what she called fun. As usual, there was no getting out of it. This time my family was on its way to a large house outside Aldeburgh. There I would be deposited with a splendid old dear whom Peggy-Ann had met on the train from Liverpool Street (a consequence of travelling posh class). She was called Letty Gifford and it turned out that she had a friend called Ethel Sunderland-Taylor who lived in an equally huge house right on the river and that they'd both welcome some company for the summer. I was a sickly child and the air would do me good, apparently. Quite what was so different about the air in this part of Suffolk as opposed to that breathed at The Old Parsonage remains unclear.

So plans were made and delivery of the boy arranged. Inspiration struck Peggy-Ann *en route*. The family canoe was already strapped to the roof rack of our battered estate car. *What fun! The older boys can go by boat!* (My sisters were somehow immune from the scheme, while my younger brother seemed a babe in arms compared with me at ten and twelve-year-old Roddy.)

The three brothers: me, Tom and Roddy, circa 1974.

The fact that it was almost dark and threatening to be a thoroughly horrible evening didn't sway her in the slightest. It was jolly well going to be fun.

Nobody protested. It was partly because resistance was useless. But also because there was something ultimately convincing about our mother's enthusiasm. Who wants to miss out on the possibility of a Great Adventure, however terrifying in prospect? So Roddy and I were duly unloaded at Snape Bridge, along with a map and a canoe, and we were left to make our own way to Cob House.

Once the car was out of sight, there were no lights visible on the estuary. In fact, there was no sign of human life anywhere to be seen. We listened to the wind.

Better set off then, we resolved. Roddy in front, me behind.

It was simple enough at first, although the water was not as flat and calm as it had seemed from up on the bridge. But at least the river stayed narrow here, with tall reeds on either side, and there was still a little daylight. The thickness of the reeds both softened and amplified the wind and the high tide was falling, which made paddling easy. At our backs, the half-ruined buildings of the old Maltings were outlined against the lighter western sky. Away from Snape then, we paddled east, along a narrow channel heading towards Iken Cliffs.

Soon the river widened. A string of reed islands formed a large lagoon to the south, but we deliberately stuck to the channel close to the northern shore. Although a short cut across the lagoon looked the quicker route, there was little deep water there, even for a canoe, and we knew that to go aground on a falling tide would lead to difficulties. Concealed posts could hole the canvas and sink us in no time. The channel should be easy to navigate, though, clearly marked by the spindly sticks called withies, faithfully maintained by the old harbourmaster at Iken. We also knew that we could make the most of the ebbing tide only if we stayed in the deep water where the current flowed fastest. We were definitely not duffers, I silently reminded myself. We wouldn't drown.

We stopped chatting, and gave ourselves over to the sound of dipping paddles and the wind in the reed beds.

This was proper wilderness. Not another person for miles, not even a house or farm. Just the grey river, and the big grey sky. After half a mile or so the river turned south to meander through another swaying reed archipelago, towards the anchorage on Cliff Reach. The wind was coming from the north, chilly, and what a sailor calls fair, so the canoe glided along at quite a pace, wind and tide working together. Roddy and I settled into a rhythm with our paddles. Dip, pull, lift. There was some comfort in the regular sloshing of water beneath the canvas.

Dip, pull, lift.

Dip, pull, lift.

Sensing the isolation, I began to worry a little about the approaching darkness. I looked at my elder brother's back and felt a little braver.

How long now, Rod? Are we nearly there?

I don't fucking know, all right. I haven't got a fucking clue where we are, but we sure as shit aren't near Aldeburgh yet.

He answered without stopping paddling. Roddy was pissed off and cold and clearly wondering why the hell he hadn't refused to do this. He turned and looked at me over his shoulder, fixing me in the eye with a glare. We put up our paddles briefly and for a moment we were left floating in stillness. Then the background rhythm of gusts in the reeds reasserted itself. Again Roddy looked right into my eyes, but this time he grinned.

We'll be OK. Come on, don't you worry. Won't be too long, I don't reckon.

And he hit a splash with his paddle and we both laughed. I splashed him back, but only lightly because I liked this levity and I didn't want a thump.

Dip, pull, lift.

Dip, pull, lift.

Another mile into our journey, and I had never felt so cold and tired in my life. Whatever excitement had been there to begin with was long gone. No matter how much we tried to keep dry, it was quite impossible. In a canoe it's always wet. There's the puddle of muddy water sloshing around inside the boat – probably a small leak. Feet and bum get soaked first. Then, as you paddle, salt water dribbles down your forearm and into your sleeves, stinging your skin.

The water was choppy, which made us wetter. From time to time Roddy caught a crab, missing the peak of a wave and scooping his paddle down into its trough so it was whipped backwards, the lack of resistance taking him by surprise. The resulting splash often hit me square in the face. More water ran down my neck, soaking my collar. As we reached open water the waves grew bigger than the little canoe, breaking over the bow and sending a spray over both of us.

The tide fell to expose expanses of flat grey mud, where waders gathered on the shores and in the reeds and called to one another. East coast estuaries have their own sound. It's strange and eerie. As we ploughed on into the gathering darkness, the calls of the peewit and the dunlin and the noises of a hundred other hidden birds and creatures combined with the water and the mud and the wind and the reeds to send a shiver through me.

At Iken Cliff we stuck to the southerly shore and it was here, in the failing light, that I first saw the vast blasted oak looming up from the bank. It stood alone in the reeds, black and solid against the huge Suffolk sky. Two birds, doves by the look of them, were sitting in the tree, almost, but not quite silhouettes.

One dove, the larger of the two, sat slightly taller. Was this the male? His head was up as if on guard, and he perched proud on the bare branch. His mate had fluffed up big and cosy and she was settled so low on the branch you couldn't see her feet. In for the night, snug and determined against the cold. The pair of birds weren't touching, but Mr Dove was turned towards Mrs Dove, and their beaks nearly met. There was a tenderness about him. He seemed to be sheltering her.

As I watched them, it struck me that we shared something with those birds, the two of us, my brother and me. Pausing in my paddling, I gazed at the doves, absorbing every detail. The sky, the old blasted oak, the changes in the spaces between the two birds as we glided by. And now they were behind me, and I twisted my neck to keep them in sight. It felt like leaving friends, but I thought of supper, and knew we couldn't stop.

The canoe glided on.

We came through Iken. The chart calls this bit Troublesome Reach, upper and lower. Troublesome it might be by sail, but in a canoe it was easy to navigate. Soon the squat tower of Iken Church came looming up through the gloom, jutting out on its peninsula.

Hard a-starboard, lads!

And we turned north into a squall.

The river was close to a mile across here and the water was sluicing eastward at speed, thoroughly choppy and angry. A tussle of wind against tide. We were soon utterly drenched. Roddy's fury at the elements was vocal and loud. But still at the back of the canoe, soaking and cold and certainly very scared, I felt a curious sense of detachment. It was like watching myself in a film. A disaster movie, even. Here we were, cast adrift on a vengeful sea, facing death and destruction. But that didn't matter. Nothing could really go wrong with my brother there to look after me. And anyway, I didn't have to go on watching this scary film if I didn't want to. I could just drift back to the two doves I'd seen, and huddle up with them. All it took was a little effort of the imagination and I could be cosy as anything, wrapped in a feather blanket, up in my blasted old oak.

The channel itself is visible only at low water. Just a few yards wide, it twists and turns incomprehensibly through a vast expanse of mud flats. You wouldn't see it at all at high water if it weren't for the withies, and these are hard to spot in the best of lights. In the dark, we had lost the channel completely. Turning the canoe east again, we ploughed on for another hour or two into an empty blackness where sky invisibly met water.

Church Reach. Bagnold's Reach. Long Reach. Past Ham Creek which leads up to Little Japan with its sandy beach and old ruined cottage. Then Collier's Reach and Blackthorn – we were there! We'd travelled a good six miles down the river and now there was a new sound gusting against the wind. The two of us boys shouting and laughing at the top of our voices.

Fuck you! You fucking bastards!

And we roared with laughter.

SHIT! FUCK! BOLLOCKS!

There was a light on the northern shore. Tiny Cob Island had appeared.

BOLLOCKS–ARSES–FUCK!

A roar of laughter and we splashed one another with the paddles, giddy with the freedom of knowing we couldn't be heard. We weren't sure if we were cursing the grown-ups or the river. Either would have been appropriate. A final salute of two fingers in the air and we headed in towards the shore. The dilapidated jetty was where it should have been but the tide had gone out so far that we felt the canoe brush the bottom and had to hop out, shoes in hand. The mud squelched wonderfully between my toes. Solid, if not dry, land.

We slithered the boat across to the jetty and tied her up. The shell-spiked mud turned to clumps of grassy reeds and then into gravelly sand. I stood on the shore, and grinned at my brother. We had made it.

Cob House was set much higher and some way off, though in the darkness we had no way of knowing that. Barefoot, we walked tentatively on the stony path leading up from the river through the long garden, relishing the softness of the damp grass once we were through the wooden gate.

We hadn't been forgotten completely. Someone had left an outside light on. Otherwise this huge pink house, curving round its garden, was utterly still and dark. No reception party. Certainly no supper.

Hey! At least they've put a tent up.

I wormed into the sleeping bag beside my brother and drifted unstoppably into sleep. The canvas rustled softly. The cry of a few last remaining waders carried on the wind, and the pull of the tide sucked the river out over grey mud, out towards the sea.

Next morning I woke at dawn. I lay on my back listening to the coo-cooing of the pigeons, before untying the tent flaps to get look at them, sleeping bag dragging like a maggot behind me. Not two pigeons, but two doves. Of course. Their call is slightly higher, more

Debbie in *Titmouse* on the river Deben near Woodbridge in the early 1960s.

reedy and sing-song. Coo-cooo coo. Two of them were sitting up high in the branches of a living oak tree, half-hidden in the green leaves. Side by side. Kneeling in my sleeping bag, I cupped my hands into a box shape, thumbs bent in front, and put my lips to my knuckles to blow out my dove whistle – a variation of my owl call. Coo-cooo coo! And a fist hit me right in the stomach.

Shut up and go back to sleep will you?

Eventually I did. But the doves stayed in my mind.

It's dark outside now and the rain is heavier. My new sketchbook lies open in front of me and I haven't drawn a thing. An older one is open at a page I drew twenty-five years ago. Two birds – not as clear as I'd like – are scratching about for food. A note underneath reads *Quails V&A 1986*.

What I'm after now is half there already, in my mind's eye. It's winter, the birds are on a branch and it's bloody freezing. A cold wind blows from the north. One dove is settled in for the night, puffed up, neck drawn in and huddled low, nice and snug. The other is standing slightly more alert, keeping an eye out for her. They don't touch, but there is definitely something between them: a relationship of trust and affection, and that's what I'm trying to capture. It's there in these quails, too.

I push back my chair and search the bookcase, gathering together a pile of dog-eared bird books: *A Field Guide to the Birds of Britain, All the Birds of the Air* and *Thorburn's Birds*. Old friends. I used to save up my pocket money and order these from catalogues. I covered them in clear plastic to protect them from the rain and wrote my name on the inside cover, carefully and always in full: Alexander John Monroe, The Old Parsonage. Tel. Woolverstone 380. Now I smile at my childish handwriting and the unforgettable phone number.

Spreading everything around me on my desk in the studio, I begin to draw the scene. Some come out OK, I think. I can draw a dove as easy as pie and I'm happy with the way I get them to puff up against the cold. But this isn't something I can describe properly in line alone. I need to go into the workshop and start making.

I know I need to narrow my choice down to a single pair of birds. Starting afresh a day later, I redraw my favourite sketches in profile. I scan and resize them on a sheet of A4, starting big and gradually reducing them in size to tiny specks. The two doves I like best are about 11mm long. I cut them out and stick these minute drawings onto a sheet of silver, 3.5mm thick, turn to look for my piercing saw and suddenly realise I'm starving. I nip back into the office and find a packet of liquorice allsorts. Stuffing my mouth with three of them, I turn round to see a beautifully dressed woman coming towards me. Just as I try to say hello a half-chewed allsort escapes and falls down my front. She's a buyer from an uptown boutique and I think I've made a bad impression. Black-toothed liquorice excuses made, I retreat back to the workshop.

Looking at it again, I know I'm not quite there yet. So I tidy my bench and it strikes me that what I really need is a cup of tea. But the buyer's still in the way so I can't go and make one. I'll have to start cutting out after all. New saw blades. I need new saw blades. I go and look in the drawer for some 4.0s. I usually use a very thin 6.0 but this is a particularly thick bit of silver so I need a thicker 4.0. None in the drawer. I'm not using a bloody 3.0 so I settle for a new pack of 5.0s.

The smell of hot light bulbs and wood begins to rise. With silver as solid as this, I turn the job, not the blade, gently curving round the breast and up to the neck and the beak. As I cut, the blade nicks at the wooden support pin and a little sawdust mingles with the silver. The radio plays Sham 69.

Hersham boys, Hersham boys, laced-up boots and corduroys . . .

I haven't heard this for a while.

I look at my birds and I'm disappointed by a niggling doubt at the back of my mind. It's getting late. Tomorrow I'll pay a visit to my old friends and see if they can help. It might set my mind at ease.

Saturday morning finds me springing up the steps in through the great arch of the Victoria and Albert Museum, hand in hand with my kids. I'm looking for the tiny exhibit in my sketchbook, which has haunted me ever since I first fell in love with it as a student. It's in the Japanese department – a little carved toggle. Seeing it in the flesh again should make all the difference. And it's time I introduced it to my daughters.

Returning with the girls, I see the museum through their eyes, exciting and unfamiliar, just as I once encountered it myself. I enjoy the wonderful feeling of anticipation aroused by the grand entrance. The strident noise of traffic on the Cromwell Road cross-fades into a hushed chatter of hundreds of voices and shuffling feet.

Come on, let's go straight to the Japanese room!

I know the way. Straight across the entrance hall with its beautiful mosaic floor and incredible ceilings, writhing green and blue glass Chihuly chandelier suspended in the dome. Eyes everywhere. Up, down, side to side, we peer through to a tempting corridor of classical Indian sculptures and down towards the medieval ironwork. No! Not the shop! We turn a sharp right, speed through China and here we are in Japan. Away from the brightness and into a dark and subdued room, with not a soul to disturb us.

The new-found silence reduces us to whispers. Whole suits of armour are here, brought to life by long white whiskers which descend from iron masks. Lacquered boxes, kimonos, and so many pots. Golden chrysanthemums gleam from the patinated bronze of an indigo-coloured vase. But there, right down at the end of the room, a little to the right, we spot a terraced set of shelves laden with exquisite little figures, made of walrus tusk, boxwood, agate and walnut.

The kids love them. I knew they would. There's something endlessly compelling about these miniature carvings, originally so practical. They were made to be toggles – two hundred, three hundred years ago – to hang a pouch from a kimono sash by a silken cord. Traditional Japanese gowns had no pockets. Some of these toggles were fashioned from ivory, some from black ebony or warm brown wood: two funny men wrestling, a sleepy rabbit, a white skull without a jaw, a perfect tiny pumpkin. But where are my birds? Not here. We look harder.

Round the back of the cabinet we find more carvings. And here are my friends, between an eagle and an owl, carved in ivory with blackened detailing, standing about an inch tall. 'Quails and Millet'. Signed: Okatori.

The carving looks exactly as I remembered it, just like the little sketch I made in my notebook twenty-five years earlier. But I need more detail now. Two little quails are perched on . . . what? A ribbon? The ground? That must be the millet under their feet – long curving leaves with a central stripe, looping round bursting seed heads. The birds are chubby and full of character and beautifully carved, but what has always fascinated me is the way they stand. They face each other, barely touching, and nearly, but not quite, side by side. The head of the slightly smaller bird is lowered, while the larger of the two looks up and over her wings. Just keeping an eye out.

The kids are soon distracted by all the other carvings. So we play a game and try to spot more by the same maker. We only find one, a tiger, one of the twelve East Asian zodiac animals. I admire its snarl but it's still the birds that I feel most drawn to. They haven't lost their charm for me. While the girls compare their finds, I do a few new sketches.

I can't help wondering about Okatori-san and how he had made them. And what he was thinking about while he carved. I sense a connection to this craftsman from Kyoto. (His older brother was a carver too, one of the greatest.) The story he'd told some two centuries before I was born still feels familiar. It's about a particular relationship, a suggestive angle, a protective gaze. It's a tale in miniature that can be told in ivory or in gold. It's the residue of a distant memory unaltered by time.

Ethel Sunderland-Taylor was a game old bird. She had a huge telescope in one of her many upstairs rooms, commanding a terrific view of the river from Iken Marshes to Westrow Point. The house also had a lift, the first we boys had ever seen.

Luckily, Ethel took a shine to me, which was reciprocated, and in the end I spent many summers living with her in that large house overlooking the Alde. It was half a mile away from Cob House, where Letty lived – the lady from the train. An eccentric elderly couple, Ethel and Letty were as fit as fiddles. They kept ornamental ducks and chickens and they shot their own dinner.

That first summer my family drove off leaving me standing by the back door, perfectly happy, still in shorts and scratchy pullover, wet shoes replaced by wellies. Just as scruffy as I was, Letty and Ethel lived in cord slacks, faded smocks and quilted Barbours, Ethel with long white hair up in a messy bun. Letty had a husband somewhere. I never actually saw him but understood that he was terribly rich. I pictured him in a darkened room, watching the cricket. Ethel was a widow who had spent a good deal of her life in India. Our evenings were spent cooking elaborate curries, carefully grinding each exotic spice by hand. I had never heard their names before. Turmeric, dhaniya, kala jeera. Beautiful rich yellows, oranges, reds and intense browns.

Occasionally a friend from Aldeburgh would visit. Letty and Ethel knew Imogen Holst and Peter Pears and Benjamin Britten. My mother remembers me playing tennis with Britten, though I have no memory of the match. As far as I was concerned, the most exciting of Letty's visitors by far was Queeny, a retired pirate who lived on a boat. Sporting canvas slacks and a sailing smock, she smoked cigars and wore a monocle. *Lorks-a-lummy*, they all cried as they chatted in the kitchen, hoots of laughter rising and cigar smoke filling the room to mingle with curry scents and the smell of wet dogs straight from the river. They reminisced about the Empire and about being torpedoed by U-boats on the North Atlantic route in the war. They discussed the problem of the fox who had taken some chickens a few nights before, and how best to shoot it. And they talked ducks. I just listened as I ground the colourful spices and breathed in their mysterious odours.

I've got a treat for you, Ethel told me on my first day there.

Upstairs – I took the lift, of course – Ethel pulled out a brace of shotguns. The smaller of the two was an ancient single bore.

Right-ho Alex, this one is yours. Ever used a shotgun before? This one is a four-ten, perfect for a skinny boy like you. There are rules, you know. Come on, you'll soon get the hang of it.

Ethel explained that she hung on to the guns in case of unwelcome intruders, animal or human. Just last week someone had been poking about in the dead of night. She shot him fair and square with rock salt and by the sound of his screams neither he nor anyone else would be back for a while. But she'd keep the twelve bore beside her bed just in case. I immediately planned to sleep with my gun too and hoped I'd soon get the chance to shoot an intruder.

The first practice shot knocked me over backwards. But there was indeed a technique and I soon mastered it. At ten years old, you can't imagine anything better than your own shotgun. Up at the crack of dawn before Ethel woke, I would make my way through the woods to my favourite spot, a grassy clearing with undergrowth behind. Here I would lie for hours, as quiet as could be, not moving a muscle until the wood itself forgot I was there. The sun slowly rose, sending long, low shafts of light through the dewy mist. Birds and insects wandered by, or flew through the wet grass, and sometimes deer appeared, and none of them saw me. Spiders spun webs, and rabbits came to feed.

I bided my time.

The animal wandered closer.

Nibbling. Listening. Nibbling.

So close now I couldn't even breathe. Squeeze, don't pull, gently, gently . . . and suddenly everything would change. Nature disappeared in the explosion. All that was left behind was the dead rabbit. There was pride and there was horror in this. Too late I always remembered how much I preferred the moments before the kill to the reality of its aftermath. But the rabbit curry would be delicious.

Just upstream from Ethel's house, and accessible only by boat, there was another magical spot called Little Japan. A small sandy beach faced south, a maze of creeks running off it into the reeds. Once it was used for loading barges with produce, but all that remained now was a broken-down old cottage tucked away in the woods. Trees grew out through its windows and it reminded me of the Hansel and Gretel story. It made a perfect hideout. I used to take my sketchbook and my shotgun, and I spent hours there, drawing avocet and dunlin (up-curved scimitar beaks and black-patched bellies), and snoozing on the warm sand. I explored the creeks, and returned with our supper when I could.

Time was marked by the rising and falling of tides as the days passed by. At Little Japan I lay on my back in the dappled shade, looking up into the branches of an ancient oak, searching for the pair of doves I could hear.

Back at my bench on Monday morning, I'm clearer about what I'm doing. I know exactly how to recreate the tenderness I remembered in that pair of quails. I have two flat cut-outs of my doves on my bench and I need to file them into shape. As usual, I solder an extra piece on to the tail of each bird, something to hold on to, a little rod for a handle, 2 inches long.

I start to file, and then to grind the silver with a small flexible micro-motor. The job gets hot and burns my fingers as I whittle away. Soft lad has been doing too much desk work recently.

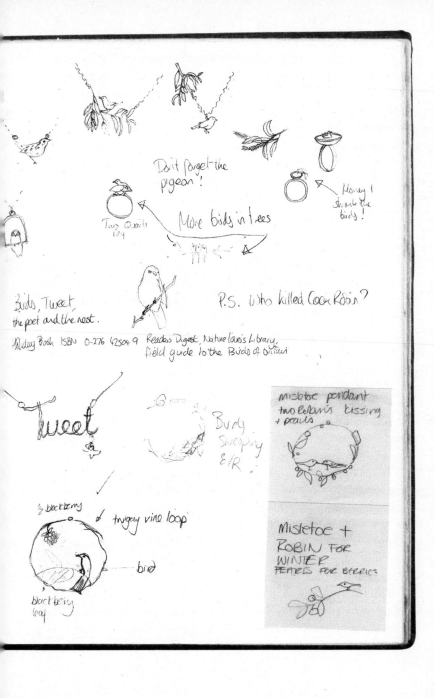

Don't forget the pigeon!

Two Quails ing

More birds in trees

Money! Shrunk the birds!

Birds, Tweet, the poet and the nest.

P.S. Who killed Cock Robin?

Holiday Book ISBN 0-276 42504 9   Readers Digest, Nature Lover's Library, field guide to the Birds of Britain

Tweet

Birdy Swooping &/R.

Mistletoe pendant
two Robin's kissing
+ pearls

½ blackberry

twiggy vine loop

bird

blackberry leaf

Mistletoe +
ROBIN FOR
WINTER
PETALS FOR BERRIES

To start with, I cannot find the forms in the metal. I file away at the silver in the hope that my dove is in there somewhere and will appear soon. But this bird is shy and reluctant and doesn't want to be seen. I decide to pull out my bird books again and prop dove pictures all around my bench. That's better.

Once again I cut and I file and I cut some more and at last it starts to take shape. I'm ready to use a different tool, a tiny ball fraizer, which always makes me think of a dentist's drill. This cuts away at the details and brings forth wings and eyes and feathers. By late afternoon a small fat bird is looking up at me. I'll leave her there for now and make a start on the larger one.

I am much bolder with my second bird and I rip into him with confidence and a coarse file. Then I have to tell myself to slow down. I'm in danger of slipping and messing up everything if I keep going at this pace. So I take a breath and put the brakes on. It's hard because I know I need to keep the momentum going.

Cocky himself, he responds to my cockiness.

I stop for a cup of tea and I ache all over but I feel I'm getting somewhere.

The next step is the branch. Then it's on to the forge to solder them into position. It doesn't go entirely to plan but I think it'll work. I fix the smaller bird first and I file away the branch to fit her really low and snug. Then the larger bird goes on. By seven o'clock they're finished and I feel fairly exhausted.

It's wintery, there's definitely something going on between the two. Perhaps it's a kind of tension but it's very endearing, and there's a lot of love in it too. I'm pleased with the angle of the twig, and the bends work very well. I need to fit the chain, and perhaps think about setting a little diamond in the piece, but I'm out of steam now so I'll finish it off tomorrow.

Looking at them for the last time before I lock up, thinking about where and how the jump rings should connect to make the necklace hang just right, I realise there is something rather lonely about my pair of turtle doves. I'm glad. If I had framed them in a circle as I've done before, they would have felt too safe, protected. This way, they seem slightly raw and exposed. And that is exactly what I wanted.

A few months after Christmas a letter arrives from the woman who'd bought those doves in our virtual trunk show. She had given the necklace to her daughter Lydia, and she wanted to tell me why. There's a scene in Lydia's favourite childhood film in which a little boy gives his meagre savings to a toyshop owner who is raising money for a children's hospice. In gratitude, the shopkeeper gives the child a pair of white turtle dove Christmas decorations, and explains their symbolism: love and unbroken friendship. The significance of that scene was sealed for Lydia by her mother's gift of my necklace.

That was when I knew that my little doves had taken off on a new life of their own. Now they were at the heart of a different story, woven around them by a different person. And that too was exactly what I wanted.

Calabria

I lie on my bed in a hotel room in Peshawar watching *Carry On Up the Khyber* on my laptop. Shot in Snowdon – from time to time you can see the steam of the actors' breath – the landscape of the film bears little resemblance to what I'd glimpsed of the Pass a few days earlier. Not that we had got very far, of course. The famous route through the mountains to Afghanistan was far too dangerous, and we had to content ourselves with photographing the fort guarding its entrance, before beating a rapid retreat from the heat. It's the very height of summer.

On my screen, Sir Sidney Ruff-Diamond (Sid James) continues to dine under descending clouds of plaster dust. He winces at the pop of a champagne cork, oblivious to the explosions going on all around him. I sweat, sprawling on my beige sheets, trying to ignore the peeling green wallpaper and overpowering smell of stale cigarette smoke, badly disguised by cheap air freshener. Perhaps a 'no smoking' room was too much to ask for at a place which had so recently been bombed itself.

Westerners are still very much a target in Pakistan, and as far as I could see, my colleague Claudia Martin and I are the only ones around. We are here on an EU mission to support the jewellery sector in Pakistan, touring the country, advising local jewellers, delivering lectures and teaching as we go along. Our guide and translator is Mr Wali, a gentle, softly spoken Ismaili from Hunza. We arrived to find a thriving industry that needed nothing from us but funds to buy equipment. The only thing we can't offer.

Karachi has grown used to the huge amounts of aid being sloshed round by the Americans. This made for a somewhat hostile reception for a couple of penniless jewellery designers with good intentions from London. But here, up-country in Peshawar, we find our audiences far more receptive. Their expectations are lower and appreciation is warm, particularly for Claudia's expertise as a gemologist.

There's always a plentiful supply of uncut gemstones coming over the borders here, most of them from Afghanistan. Pakistan itself is a mineral-rich country with a good supply of tourmaline, peridot, topaz and aquamarine and Peshawar has developed a busy stone-cutting industry. But without investment, tools and conditions are still rudimentary. Stones can be cut more cheaply and accurately in India.

I love this city at the crossroads of the world, and I'm excited, if occasionally alarmed, by its frontier feel. Later that hot night we lie out on the roof of the hotel on rope-strung wooden beds called *charpois*, while sweet cardamom tea is brewed for us in a chipped enamel teapot over the grate of an open fire. A Pashto musician plucks his *rebab* while another drums out a hypnotic rhythm on a small *dhol* drum. Then Mr Wali arrives with news. A party of Afghan smugglers have recently arrived in town with a good selection of gemstones, including some spectacular emeralds. Were we interested? Claudia has a professional curiosity and I think it might be a good opportunity to buy some stones for a commission waiting for me back in London. We arrange to meet them the following morning.

After a breakfast of bread and fresh mango juice, we find Mr Wali waiting for us in the lobby, with Mr Ali, our local advisor. Mr Ali, an extremely dignified young man who has grown up in the Peshwari lapidary business, is both knowledgeable and highly skilled as a cutter himself. He also teaches, which gives him a special status in the community, and has connections with the Gems and Gemological Institute of Pakistan.

Our taxi cannot penetrate far into the Afghan quarter of the city before the driver is defeated by the lively labyrinth of narrow streets. We happily get out and walk. Women dressed like coloured shuttle-cocks look away through narrow gauze eye-slits. Ancient, high, crumbling walls are festooned with hanging cloths, scarves and dresses drying in the sun. Exposed cables and electrical wires run anarchically over our heads. We encounter more than one mournful-looking donkey, patiently waiting among piles of sand as street-workers dustily shovel rubble into sacks slung across its back. Protected from the sun by a cloth, a great basket of vegetables passes by, balanced on the head of a bearded man in a baby-blue *shalwar kameez*. He also carries a huge bunch of bananas in each hand.

The further we go, the more fantastic the architecture becomes, the buildings reaching such a state of disintegration it's a wonder they still stand. From intricately carved balconies, the palatial remains of a colonial era, pale sheets of material are strung across from side to side, bannerlike, for shade. Turning left through a high archway, we find ourselves a large, light, open space. It is a covered bazaar, tiled in the most amazing patterns, radiating blue floral designs on a white background with red and gold detailing. Here and there the pretty tiles have been brutally smashed through to admit yet another tangle of wiring.

All kinds of Afghan wares are being sold from the glass-fronted stalls around the edge of the market. Delicate glass phials which are probably less ancient than they look, old tiles, collections of antique brass and copper, brilliantly coloured cloths with beads and mirrors sewn into their designs. Afghan jewellery too, which has a rather different style from its gaudy Pakistani cousin. I quickly get out my notebook to scribble a few sketches. Lapis lazuli is the favourite stone, intensely blue in a setting of tarnished silver, though I also see a black stone which I guess is agate, and tiny wooden beads strung in combination with minute silver balls. My eye and my pencil are caught by a silver cylinder hanging horizontally from one string of these beads. It is almost bullet-shaped, cone-ended, and about the size of a lipstick. One end, secured by a safety chain, comes off to reveal a secret chamber, and I suddenly realise it is an amulet, designed to store a written prayer or blessing to keep its owner safe.

I don't have time to draw any other necklaces. We are led off, through more darkened passageways and heavy doors, and this time down lots of steps too. Eventually we arrive at our rendezvous, which must be well below street level.

As-Salamu Alaykum.

Wa `alaykumu as-salāmu wa rahmatullāhi wa barakātuh.

We politely remove our shoes before shaking hands and sitting down with the bearded young men on the floor, grateful for the 7-Up we are offered. While Mr Ali talks, we wait and drink and the men look at us, nodding and smiling. Their faces are kind but you can see these are hard men. Displaced by the American invasion, they are now surviving by smuggling gemstones over the Khyber Pass. They keep their guns by their side, and more are stacked against the wall.

Soon Claudia begins to ask questions about the quality of the gemstones, and how they are mined and cut. One of the men produces a soft leather pouch and tips some emeralds into the palm of her hand. They are the brightest thing in the room. I can see Claudia's eyes light up, and I'm sure mine do too. The colour is so brilliant, so strong, and they have an unusual clarity. I am used to seeing emeralds with more inclusions – marks of other minerals, liquids or gases trapped in the gemstone, which can detract from, or sometimes add, to its value.

I'm interested in buying some, I tell Mr Ali. Could he ask the price?

The dollar-per-carat weight rate he quotes means nothing to me, so I consult Claudia. She takes out her loupe – a little handle-less magnifying glass the size and shape of a dice shaker – and inspects the stones more closely. As she glances at me, she nods, almost imperceptibly. They are good stones, and so is their price.

That means it is time to haggle. I ask Mr Ali to offer less.

The atmosphere shifts. We are getting down to business now. All at once we are arguing. That is more like it. This is the best adventure I've had since arriving in Pakistan. Nothing like finding yourself cross-legged on the floor in a cellar in Peshawar with a bunch of armed Afghans, disputing the price of emeralds, to take away the taste of homesickness.

A few nights later, when it is too hot to sleep, I creep down after midnight to watch the football. England are playing in the World Cup, and a small crowd of Pakistani men are gathered around a large television next to a stage in the white marble hotel lobby. The place is depressingly nondescript, all white marble and fake statues and brash gold trimmings. Mindful of my warning to avoid groups like this, which are prime targets for bombings, Westerners offering an added attraction, I carefully refrain from cheering when England scores. But I can't pretend I blend in.

The feeling of not being sure if you'll be blown up is much more uncomfortable than I remember it. I find it's always better if you have no idea what's coming.

I had already devised an elaborate system of tripwires along the approaches to the orchards and the main gardens of the house, honing my technique carefully over the years. About 2 inches above ground level, a line of tarred twine was strung across the path. This was fed around a cotton-reel pulley, and then attached to the trigger: a tapered plug, forced into a short retainer-stake already driven into the ground. A crossbow was fixed to the ground too, its string pulled back onto the retainer-stake, and the trigger-plug gently pushed home to retain the taut crossbow string. The whole affair was then camouflaged with grass and leaves. If you tripped the wire, out came the plug, ping went the string, and the arrow shot out. You were done for. Or so we hoped.

The choice of bolt, or arrow, depended on the target. Fights with the boys we knew from our village primary school were prearranged, and rules applied. We tended to ambush them with coppiced hazel arrows, stripped of bark and sharpened to a point. Considerable effort was invested in making these. Trimmed pigeon feathers were bound in place with twine for flights, and we often used to cut away the bark in elaborate banded patterns. We had a reasonable chance of getting some of these arrows back.

Other adversaries we had to take more seriously. For as long as I could remember, we had been defending ourselves from the boys of Woolverstone Hall. Known to us simply as The Enemy, they used to sneak into our gardens to scrump apples, or take a peek at the girls as they blossomed: both Debbie and Nikki were very pretty teenagers, and ever-more tempting. If the intruders encountered Roddy or me, they showed no mercy. During the worst of his many beatings, as he lay pinned to the ground while a Hall boy repeatedly jumped on his head, Roddy thought he would probably die. So when it came to The Enemy, it was open war.

The Hall, a magnificent Palladian mansion standing less than a mile from The Old Parsonage, was a London County Council experiment – a state-run residential grammar, at least until 1977. Closer to a boarding school than an Approved School, many of Woolverstone Hall's pupils were there because their parents were away in the forces, but the place also had its fair share of tearaways and magistrate referrals, bright inner city boys who had learned to be tough from an early age. There was much talk of 'broken homes' in those days. One of the boarding houses, Corner's – a beautiful Lutyens building with Gertrude Jekyll gardens, heartlessly converted – lay in precisely the opposite direction from us, the cinder path between school and boarding house running right past our back gate. This gave The Enemy ample opportunities for attack, and us to retaliate.

Clearly, the Hall inmates required something more lethal than hazel. For the real Enemy, we reserved our bamboo bolts. A metre long, these were weighted at the front with 6-inch nails. We simply removed the nail heads and pushed the shafts, pointed end out, into the hollow of the bamboo. Choose the right feather flights, and these arrows flew fast and true.

The real skill lay in their positioning. There was an art in judging where to aim, and this was both the joy and the frustration of our booby traps. The Enemy would be coming from the direction of the river, of course. But they came in all sizes. Best to aim somewhere around hip-height. At what speed would they approach? We calculated for a fast walk. By a mixture of trial and error, and systematic testing with dummy bolts and volunteers on the path, we became pretty accurate, though we often found that bows had been tripped with no sign of a direct hit. Occasionally we would hear a cry in the night, or we'd peek round the kitchen door to see a strange boy in blood-soaked flares at the big table, Debbie or Nikki gently bathing a wound. Once a rather nice older boy limped in with a whole arrow embedded in his leg. He'd been visiting one of my sisters, by arrangement, and had made the mistake of coming through the back gardens at night. He may have been a boyfriend, but he was still a Hall boy and that made him a legitimate target.

I'm afraid I recently ran into one of the few we actually befriended ourselves, now a middle-aged father of three. He pulled up his shirt to show me two scars, entry and exit wounds from a long-forgotten battle. I squirmed with horror, and apologised profusely. He bore no grudge.

The jewellery workshops in downtown Peshawar are stiflingly hot. They are hidden away in the oldest part of the city, down alleys and passages as dark and winding as tunnels. We are taken to one tiny high-ceilinged room after another, where men and young boys are hard at work in conditions that seem quite impossible to me. High narrow windows mean there is little in the way of natural light, with only a dusty light bulb hanging unshaded from a long frayed flex to compensate. Craftsmen dress in light cotton *shalwar kameez* and work on the floor, sitting on stained, buff-coloured scraps of carpets at low tables. No women, ever. Dirty walls painted apple green or tiled up

By the time I return home from Pakistan, I am dying to get back into my workshop and experiment with plasticine. But it is high summer and that means flying straight off to Calabria in southern Italy for a holiday with my family. Just where you would tie the lace on the boot of Italy, there's a little coastal village called Acquappesa, an hour or so north of Cosenza. The old village, Acquappesa Paese, is scattered up the steep rocky hillside and has been half abandoned. The new village is strung along a narrow strip between the railway track and the sea. It's not the prettiest place in Italy but it has a decayed, old-fashioned charm, and I've never met another English person there in all the years we've known it. The water and electricity are turned off at regular intervals, and villagers meet around a standpipe to fill buckets so they can cook supper. From time to time, everyone brings chairs down to the square by the church and they project a movie onto its crumbling stone walls. We stay in one of Donna Vittoria's *appartamenti*, wedged between the railway line (with heavy freight trains thundering by every few hours) and the promenade (where young men and women walk and chat into the small hours). But it's the heat, not the noise, that keeps you awake at night.

Get up early enough, while it's still cool, and you can take a path up to the old town through a gap in the buildings opposite the church. It's the most direct route, and extremely steep, but it's been officially closed for years because of the instability of the giant stone steps and the poisonous snakes that lie out basking on them. The alternative, a new path which winds its way up the hillside in a more leisurely fashion, leads off to the right by an old mulberry tree whose irresistible fruit leaves your fingers stained with thick crimson juice. It's a good place to draw. Instead of the bright showy bougainvillea, hibiscus and amaryllis planted down in the coastal village, up here you can find all sorts of interesting wildflowers and leaves to sketch, and treasures like seed heads or dead insects. I have no idea of the names of most of them, but I sketch away in the shade of the mulberry tree until the sun gets too hot. And then I head down for a dip in the treacherous sea.

★

As soon as we are back in London, I start planning the new collections for Spring/Summer 2007. Inspired by what I'd seen in Pakistan, I decide to skip the drawing stage of design for once. I wonder what will happen if I design as I make, experimenting with the techniques I'd witnessed.

I buy a new packet of plasticine from the art shop. Thick-ribbed ribbons of colour, looking exactly like the plasticine of my childhood. I choose blue, which looks best against the silver, moulding a shallow dome of it straight onto my bench. Rummaging through my bits-and-bobs box, I find a little flying swallow, all sorts of tiny flowers, some minute leaves, and a filigree butterfly no bigger than a sequin, all cast-offs from previous experiments. I lay the swallow on the plasticine, pushing it down firmly, and add a few flowers. It looks OK. But I'm after the kind of swirls and tiny bobbles I saw in Peshawar. So I cut some 1cm lengths of silver wire and bend them into little swirls like sixes, using a pair of fine-pointed round-nosed pliers. Then I cut about twenty or so fragments off another piece of silver wire, chuck them on the forge and melt them into tiny shining beads. They move around as they heat up, becoming molten and excitable, one or two jumping together to form slightly larger balls. But I don't mind. I want a selection of sizes. A minute in the pickle, a hot acid solution, and they're all clean again – pearly white and shiny and ready to use. I place the twirls between the swallow and the flowers and start to work up some sort of composition, filling the little gaps with beads and leaves. The piece takes on a sort of teardrop shape, about 3cm long. I quite like it and I'm very keen to try out the soldering technique, so I decide it'll do. I use some bright yellow plasticine now to build up little retaining walls before mixing a little plaster of Paris to pour over my composition. I wait for it to set. But after a minute or two I know I'm far too impatient to take this one step at a time, so I start another piece. This one is based around the butterfly, built up on red plasticine this time, with green walls. The shape, and the swirls and bobbles it contains, combine to create the impression of paisley. I fill it up with plaster too.

Again I have to wait. This is the bit I hate most. I check the plaster, which has set, but I guess it has to be bone dry before I can solder on it. The sensible thing will be to leave both pieces overnight. I wander back to my design desk and open up my sketchbook. On a great big new blank page, I have written: *New Collections Spring/Summer 2007.*

And nothing else.

One miserable rainy afternoon in the autumn of 1972, my family decided to make a rare trip to the cinema. *The Aristocats* was playing at the Ipswich Gaumont. As usual, too many people were involved. There was another family, and lots of children, and dividing ourselves between two cars was proving problematic.

I'm not sitting next to him . . .

I want to go in the other car!

My mother drove a rusty white Mini, from which I was promptly removed because Debbie wanted her friend in the car with her. My other sister Nikki was fed up with all this and refused to come, staying at home with my father. A soft-spoken, gentle man, he never much liked the cacophony of family life and would usually find a quiet spot to avoid any disruption. Quite often, he'd take to his bed, though it was years before I found out exactly why. An expedition to the cinema was not his idea of fun. Our manly trip to see *Live and Let Die* the following year was a treat so unusual that Roddy and I have never forgotten it.

Eventually we were all squeezed into two cars and off we went, just as it was getting dark, the Mini leading the way. About halfway there, we reached a short stretch of dual carriageway, over which flickering orange street lamps cast a peculiar sodium glow. Out of the corner of my eye I caught sight of my mother's Mini just ahead. Like a slow-motion ballet dancer, the car flipped and began to spin through the air. With a terrifying crunch of metal and glass, it hit an electricity pole. Roddy and I pressed our faces to the window while we glided past the carnage in decelerating silence.

A period of chaos. We emerged from our car. A grown-up, a stranger, took me by the shoulders and looked into my eyes. His heavy hands pressed down on me as hard as they could, as if he wanted to stick me to the spot.

Don't, whatever you do, don't go over there. Don't look . . .

Then we were left alone. My brother and I stood staring across four empty lanes of road at a crumple of metal. The fallen electricity pole hung over it like a broken daffodil. In the wreckage were my mother, my sister Debbie, her friend Louise and my younger brother Tom. We could see bodies hanging out of windows from where we stood. And quite a lot of blood. They couldn't really expect us to stay where we were. We dashed across the road and up to the car, unnoticed.

What a mess, I thought, crunching through the powdered glass. It felt just like walking on sugar.

The front of the car was completely crushed in and unrecognisable. Blood and bits of flesh were mixed with metal and glass. My mother was half out through the windscreen, her door was open, and the engine seemed to be in her lap. I thought her legs had been completely chopped off. She had bitten her own tongue off. Debbie was in the front passenger seat with a spade stuck through her. It was one of those old-fashioned army shovels with a heart-shaped blade that folded up, and was kept in the car boot for digging snow. All this was far too much for a child to take in. Somehow all I could think about was how strange it was to see a car ripped open, all its workings exposed. I couldn't believe how fragile it all was. Rather like its occupants, I suppose.

As we looked, two or three large silver ball bearings plopped out from the wheel, dropping onto the oil-slicked tarmac. They made a curious muffled sound as they fell, and rolled slowly through the thick lubricant. They looked exactly like silver gobstoppers. I really wanted one.

Sirens approached, and flashing lights, and suddenly we were whisked away. Here my memory fades. Perhaps there was a blanket and a cup of sweet tea. By this time I think it was quite dark – almost pitch black, as the crash had cut off the supply of electricity to the entire area. Just headlights to see by, and the emergency vehicles' insistent flash.

When the police finally knocked on the door to tell my father about the crash, they assured him, apologetically, that nobody was likely to survive, except for my sister's friend Louise, who had relatively minor injuries. Then they offered to take him to Ipswich Hospital to see his wife and daughter. He arrived, and gazed at their motionless bodies surrounded by medics fighting to keep them alive. He must have been afraid of the answer, but he finally plucked up courage to ask about Tom.

Where's my son? Did he not survive?

The policemen looked confused. Then they seemed embarrassed. They went into a huddle and whispered to each other. Could my father hold on for a few minutes?

He was beginning to panic. The policemen probably were too.

No boy had been found at the crash. In fact, this was the first they'd heard about him. A police car was dispatched. Three-year-old Tom was only found the following morning. He had a habit of standing in front of the back seats of the car, between the two front ones. When the car had crashed he must have been flung a considerable distance through the windscreen, and right into somebody's garden. Perhaps the owners were out when the crash happened, and didn't find him till the road had been cleared. Could their phone have been out of order? Whatever the reason for the delay, they were a nice couple, and decided to keep him overnight, only calling the police the next day. He was alive and relatively well, arriving in hospital with a broken hip and a few cuts and bruises.

My mother's progress was reported each day in the local newspaper. At first they announced her condition had worsened. Things looked very bad. But then, against all expectations, both she and Debbie rallied. A few days later, their condition was reported as 'satisfactory'. They'd be in hospital for months, to be sure, but most miraculously, they were now expected to live.

At this point my father – never much in evidence before – disappeared from our lives almost completely. It must have been very hard for him. He divided his time between his architectural practice, which he ran from the cellars at The Old Parsonage (strictly out of bounds to children) and the hospital. I don't remember ever visiting the hospital myself. Perhaps they wanted to protect me; perhaps my mother was in a state too alarming to witness; perhaps the hospital had ruled that children would be too disturbing for her. But my father was there often. He must have felt even more awful because he maintained the cars himself, a perpetual process of fixing and tinkering. It was some time afterwards that we discovered that nobody could have predicted this accident: it was all down to a faulty bearing, a tiny bit of metal shattering at precisely the wrong moment.

A change came over The Old Parsonage, and it was very much for the worse. Sympathetic well-meaning ladies visited our house bringing shepherd's pies. They talked in hushed voices and looked at me in a way I found hard to interpret, but didn't much like. Some of them even tried to hug me, which I liked a good deal less. The adult world must have decided that we needed looking after. For the first time in our lives, grown-ups imposed themselves on us. It became much harder to sneak off unnoticed. Our experiments with crossbows and explosives came to an abrupt end. I began to resent my mother's absence purely because of the presence of all these other well-meaning adults.

The following spring, some time after Tom and Debbie had been discharged, my mother came home from hospital in a wheelchair, her legs a mass of metal plates and pins. At this point, thankfully, the unwanted attention waned. I was free again to escape back into my own world and I began to develop pit traps to back up the tripwires. The pits we dug were substantial, about 3 feet deep, and in highly strategic positions. We stuck sharpened stakes in the bottom, and then covered the pits with a lattice of twigs, disguised with a sprinkling of grass or leaves. I became the master of camouflage. I checked them every morning and sometimes one had been disturbed. The combination of pits and crossbows was proving effective. The Hall boys started to stay away. We were winning.

I have no idea what led me to build a pit trap for my mother the first time she walked again. She had just started getting about in the house, and then began to hobble to the orchard where we hung out the washing to dry. As there was only one path, positioning the trap was easy. I did a beautiful job. It was as good as invisible, just by the swing, which hung from an old Bramley tree. There was even a perfectly positioned bay tree, huge and capacious, where we could hide while we observed operations.

On cue, the wrought-iron gate creaked on its hinges and my mother appeared, moving gingerly. She had a walking stick in one hand and a basket in the other. She shuffled along slowly, taking two or three tiny steps at a time before repositioning her stick with caution. We held our breath as she approached the pit. Then she stopped. For what seemed like an age she looked down at the ground. Her head went up, and she scanned the orchard as if looking for us, and we shrank back in fear. But without a word, she sidestepped a few paces, then continued on her way to the line with her basket to gather in the washing.

You can't out-fox a fox.

Later that afternoon we were tracked down by Nikki and summoned into the house.

It really was too bad. What were we thinking? Our mother had been very ill. This could have been the final straw. This time we had really gone too far. And of course she was right, though why I couldn't see this at the time is beyond me. I don't think we meant to be callous. We were simply curious. Perhaps somewhere in the depths of my subconscious, I suppose I must have felt she was well enough by then to be punished for all the disruption her absence had caused, but even now I sidestep that explanation.

Anyway, things were going to have to change. Our parents intended to keep a closer eye on us. For the time being, at least, all weapons manufacturing had to be suspended.

This photograph was taken in the drawing room at The Old Parsonage
and I'm wearing my best cowboy outfit. From left to right: Roddy, me,
Nikki, Peggy-Ann, Stuart, Tom and Debbie.

I get going again on the plasticine first thing in the morning. First
things first: off come the yellow walls, and then I carefully peel back
the blue plasticine to reveal the back of the silver, each piece securely
embedded in the plaster. I'm ready to solder.

My forge is over by the sink. A jumble of firebricks is stacked on
a bench against the wall and a brazing-hearth turntable is loaded
with pieces of heatproof board, honeycomb soldering boards and
bits of charcoal blocks. The blowtorch hangs on a hook to the
right, fed by a propane cylinder under the bench. Soldering is a
jeweller's technique for attaching two pieces of metal. It's different
from welding, which melts and fuses the joint itself: if you add a

filler metal into the join, it will be the same kind. When you solder, you're melting an alloy of metals with a slightly lower melting point into the joint, and the trick is only to melt the solder, and not the pieces you're joining.

Solder, like everything else, has its likes and dislikes. It loves heat. It loves cleanliness. And it can't resist a capillary pull. But it absolutely hates grubbiness and people trying to tell it what to do. I love soldering because I have been doing it for so long we've become old friends. It is a fluid and organic process. Almost instinctive. If you know how to treat it, you can persuade the solder to do almost anything for you: get it sticky and thick to rebuild a missing petal on a flower; send it shooting along a long join, sucking its way towards the heat and defying gravity; coax it by stroking it with the flame; tempt it with a steel needle heated to white hot.

Solder comes in various guises, in different alloy mixes, each with their own specific melting point and speciality. Typically, a jeweller cuts tiny squares called pallions from a sheet, each the size of a piece of glitter, placing each one exactly where it's needed.

But for this job I'm going to cheat. No cleaning in advance, or messing about with pallions, or finding just the right pair of tweezers or forceps or pointers, which all lie jumbled in a tray beside the forge, like the tools of an unhygienic surgeon. I'm going to use syringe solder. This is a paste of ground solder in ready-made flux. (Usually you have to mix that up yourself, making a milky paste of ground borax and water, which has to be painted onto the joint before soldering to prevent oxidisation.) This special easy-flow stuff comes in a syringe so you can just squeeze it out exactly where you want it, like a tube of writing icing, and it cleans as it melts so the whole job gets stripped clean as you warm it with the torch. With about fifty joins to make, it's going to be a whole lot easier than trying to position lots of tiny pallions of solder.

When all the joins are covered in paste, I turn on my torch. This is quite a big soldering job so I need a lot of heat, and that's why I need the forge's big torch rather than the delicate needle flame

I often use. The blowtorch sparks into life with a click, blue paint-brush-shaped flame and a gentle roar. There's no skill or grace here. I just blast the plaster block from above and wait for it all to heat up. It's hot and there's an acrid smell as some of the organic material that's in the plaster burns out. I hold my face closer to get a good look. Slowly it gets hotter and the silver begins to glow red. The flux is melting now, like warm honey. Solder pings from powder to shining liquid as it runs into every join. It's done.

With a pair of tweezers I drop the whole thing into a bowl of water. The plaster fizzes and hisses like soluble aspirin and breaks up. There are still a few bits stuck to the silver so I carefully brush them away with an old toothbrush. And there it is, my teardrop composition with the swallow and flowers. I pop it into the hot pickle to clean up the metal and remove any remaining flux. Then into the barrel polisher for five minutes to shine it up some more. Finally I repeat the whole process with my other lump of plasticine.

Back at my design desk I put the two pieces on my empty sketch-book page. The swallow swoops through the teardrop, among an array of leaves and flowers, and the butterfly looks great, surrounded by swirls and bobbles in a mango-shaped flourish. The technique has worked a treat. But I quickly realise what I've known all along: it's not perfect, because I've missed a step. In my enthusiasm for the technical challenge, I've jumped straight to the making. Though I'd always intended to do part of the design on the bench, experimenting with the components on the plasticine, I've still rushed ahead too fast. I'll have to go back a step or two and start again.

I turn back a page in my sketchbook and pressed leaves and petals spill out onto my desk. I'm back in Calabria, under the mulberry tree and wandering past the vivid blooms down on the promenade.

Always start from your original research.

Two years later, despite the best of intentions, the parental ban on weapon-making had been forgotten. And with just the occasional hit, and no end of misses, the Hall boys kept coming. More fire-power was required, we decided in the summer of 1974, so I began to design ever-more-powerful crossbows. I tried using thick rubber instead of string, and multiple arrows in a single bow. Although my crossbows could inflict some impressive injuries, they were no longer a real deterrent. We needed to up the ante.

At this point our main weapons factory was in a small shed off the walled garden, next to where the coal was kept. It smelled of boiled cabbage and steam-soaked bricks because it also happened to be where I prepared the food for my ducks, boiling up leftovers in great pressure cookers each morning before school, and mixing the hot sludge with meal. It was a great place for making things, but it was no good for creative work. Research and Development took place in the Boys' Room.

A long corridor with various doors opening off it led from the flagstoned kitchen to the main hall. One of these doors took you to the back stairs, once used by the servants of the house. That was the way to the Boys' Room, tucked away by itself off a landing with a bathroom, in a part of the house that was otherwise pleasantly neglected. We shared a large room with high ceilings and exposed oak beams; a single huge, rattling sash window overlooked the walled garden. There were three beds, all built by my father, one up high in the corner with a fixed ladder. A hammock hung from the main beam. You'd often come upon a bat or two sleeping in the room during daylight hours.

It was time to investigate the possibilities of explosives. Time to move beyond arrows and bolt bombs and Lego. I began by shaving the heads off black matches and igniting little piles of the resulting powder. Next, I tried bending over the end of a piece of copper pipe, drilling a small fuse hole and pouring in my home-made gunpowder. A wad of cloth then a handful of split-shot – little lead spheres used to weight a fishing float – followed by another piece of wadding, and it was ready. Down in the duck-food shed we clamped the pipe into a vice and tied a match to a bamboo pole. Roddy lit the match, fumbled with the pole, and we quickly stood as far away as we could, wincing in anticipation as we turned away just enough to protect ourselves, but not so far that we'd miss the action. We saw a tiny spark, and another – for an instant time seemed to stop altogether – and finally there was a bigger flare, and kaboom! A huge explosion deafened us. The room filled with smoke and we tumbled out coughing, in fits of laughter and relief. Success.

It took months to get the formula perfect. We developed much faster burning powder. Once I'd developed the simple tube prototype, the device began to look more like a shotgun, complete with a carved wooden stock. Even we were rather terrified of these guns, and we only ever shot them with a long stick at a safe distance. As we improved the quality and increased the load of gunpowder, it took an ever lighter touch to explode them and this added considerably to the excitement. I also built pistols, but I was too afraid to shoot them myself. Instead, I would bribe my younger brother Tom to dress up in protective clothing, complete with an ancient crash helmet and goggles. He'd fire the pistol in his hand, and all three of us would whoop with laughter as he staggered backwards with the recoil, disappearing in a vast cloud of smoke.

But of course these guns could only be fired once. Much more efficient, I realised, would be separate bullet-cartridge cases which could be loaded into the gun for repeat shots. (I also wanted a better trigger mechanism.) Tom had bags of used 0.303 cartridges collected on visits to a ghost village in Wiltshire that had been taken over by the army for training during the war, and never repopulated. I requisitioned the whole collection. Drilling a hole in the base of the first (full metal jacket) bullet case for the fuse, I filled it with our new, improved gunpowder mix, then added wadding and shot. I built a brand-new rifle for the new ammunition. We headed out to the old boiler-house to try it out.

Our first target was an old unwanted chemistry set, still in its box. Roddy and I clamped the gun to a table opposite, then fired the gun with our trusty stick-and-match method. Spark-fizz-kaboom! Hooting with delight, we peered through the smoke. Blown to bits. Just a few scraps of cardboard were left fluttering in the air. This was the way forward.

We were soon able to make refinements. The key to a successful shot was the speed of burn. Red matches worked much better than black, and the finer you ground the powder, the quicker it burned. A few weeks later, up in the Boys' Room, I began work on a new super-gun. I had begun to suspect that the most successful bullets were the ones we had packed most tightly. After grinding the red powder as finely as I could, and filling the prepared bullet case, I began to cast around for a suitable tool that would fit precisely down the 0.303-inch neck of the bullet case and compress the gunpowder most efficiently. All I could find of exactly the right size was a drill bit from my father's workshop. It was a bad use of a precision tool and I hated doing it. But needs must. Pushing the blunt end of the bit into the bullet case, I tapped the sharp end gently with a hammer. Tap. Tap. Tap. Then I tapped a little harder. And next . . . nothing.

I didn't see that coming.

No sound, no feeling, no sensations at all. I found myself lying on my back as the ceiling swam into focus. The room was full of smoke, sweet and peppery, and a huge hole had opened up above me, plaster dust adding to the pall. I was aware of people in the room. My sisters, I realised. But still there was no noise. Very slowly, a brittle pain crept into my hands, up my arms and into my face. There was a lot of blood coming from somewhere. Detached confusion gave way to the here and now and soon things really began to hurt. I had a searing pain in my arms and a terrible ringing started up in my ears. The girls were fussing and coughing, and Nikki quickly pulled open the sash window. I tried to sit up but my body wouldn't respond. More towels arrived for the blood.

I was horrified when I realised what must have happened: the shell had exploded, firing the drill bit backwards into my head. I'd got away relatively lightly, with just a glancing blow and a nasty cut. But Roddy was down in the weapons factory, with ten or more other cartridges, following exactly the same procedure. Quick! Debbie ran down in a fury, her shouting echoing up the backstairs, and arrived just in time to put a stop to it.

For weeks afterwards, my face was peppered with explosive bright red freckles. The unburned powder had blasted into my face and embedded itself under my skin. Worried that I had become combustible, I decided to keep well away from naked flames and didn't smoke a cigarette for a fortnight.

They made us swear solemnly to stop making guns and to stop making gunpowder. Which, for a while, we did.

I start by drawing up my sketches from Italy. Then I follow the usual pattern for the components of the design – scanning and reducing the drawings before sticking them onto sheets of silver, cutting them out, constructing the flowers and plants, and texturing the leaves. The flowers have a sunny Mediterranean feel to them: trumpet-like hibiscus with long stamens, the wildflowers more stylised, with tiny beads of silver forming pistil and stamen.

So now I have a good selection of little flowers and leaves in front of me, the largest no bigger than a small button. I sketch out a few ideas from these, but I think I'm ready to start playing with the construction on my plasticine base. Remembering the Peshawar craftsmen, I press an assortment of flora into the clay, and come up with some interesting compositions. I want to do a great celebratory crescent but something seems to be missing. Returning to my sketchbook, I flick through the pages and there, mixed up with all those pressed leaves and petals, are my original experiments in silver.

It's the bird that gives the first piece that wonderful sense of movement. I take three little swallows from my bits-and-bobs box, introduce them to my crescent composition and the piece immediately comes to life.

Again, I cast plaster over the plasticine and silver, and again, I have an agonising wait.

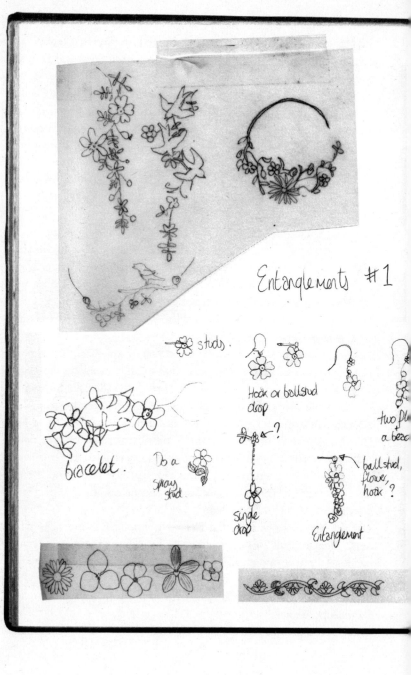

Entanglements #1

studs.

Hook or ballstud drop

two fl...
a bea...

bracelet.

Do a spray stud.

?

single drop

ballstud, flower, hook?

Entanglement

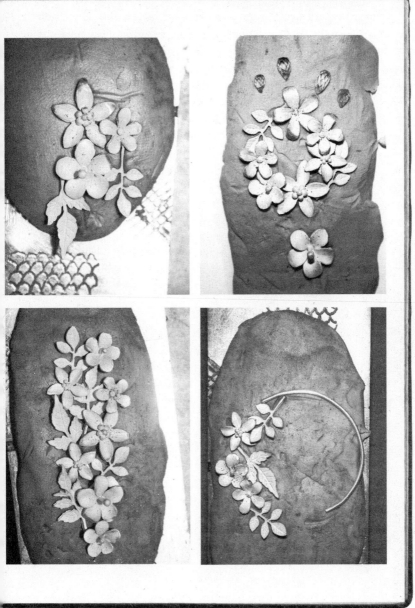

The next day I peel off the plasticine, syringe on the solder, give it a blast with the torch and hear the hiss in the water. Feeling like an archaeologist, I gently brush away the remaining plaster, hoping to find something worthwhile beneath. And there it is, a design about the size of a smile, and with the feeling of a smile too. It's a festive burst of floral. Much more Italian than Pakistani, I realise.

This collection is going to be called Calabria.

The Gardener

It's September 2009 and I'm setting up at London Fashion Week again. We are transporting everything we need to recreate a little world in miniature. An allotment in silver and gold. I know it's charming. I know it's worked before. But still I take a deep breath, fortify myself with the scent of moss and peat and seedlings and stones, and prepare for battle.

We arrive at Somerset House to find ourselves unceremoniously allocated a stand in a disused office block nearby. It's not a long walk but you do have to cross some busy roads and I'm carrying a stack of heavy wooden trays. My humour doesn't improve when I see the building. The square-panelled suspended ceiling is broken in places, and hanging cables and ducting spew out of the gaping holes. The walls are grubby. Fluorescent strip lights flicker. I have a look at the stand itself. It's the usual shell scheme design, an aluminium-framed structure with white infill panels, about a metre deep and four metres wide. For the second time in ten minutes, I trip over an odd 30cm return on one of the sidewalls. I ask a workman to remove it.

Stay calm, Alex. Try and be constructive.

There's no time to grumble. The show opens in two days and we need to get everything set up. Emma, Suzy and I crack on with the task in hand: to recreate a magical little world I've invented to display the new collection of jewellery called The Gardener. This is a collection that has evolved in a topsy-turvy sort of a way. It was my way out of a paradox.

Every season, after every show, just as I'm finally settling into relief that a collection has been well received – it's a success, even! – I am brought up short by a curious feeling of nervous anticipation. It begins in the pit of my stomach. I don't know why I don't recognise it sooner. And then I remember. It's not over, you fool. You can't relax. You have to do this all over again in six months' time. Even when you ignore the inter-season collections (which have ridiculous names like 'Cruise' and 'Pre-Fall'), each set of shows comes round too quickly. And the more successful the last collection has proved, the more anxious I immediately start to feel about the next. Because next season my buyers will be wanting more of the same. Just so long as it's completely different, of course.

Meanwhile, what ought to be an exciting whirlwind easily becomes quite overwhelming and oppressive. I also make exclusive collections for all kinds of important retailers around the world. Then there are the special events which need new and different designs too – an anniversary at Kew Gardens perhaps, or the opening of a new shop in Japan – not to mention special fund-raising pieces for charities, collaborative collections, trunk-show pieces and a mass of bespoke designs. One day I might learn to say 'no'.

Expectations create claustrophobia. But at least I have plenty of ideas in the bank. I've always got my sketchbooks. Eight tatty back-broken old A4 volumes in a bookcase in my Elephant and Castle studio office, shelved among rows of lever-arch files labelled *Orders on* or *Suppliers*. Some of these sketchbooks are neatly numbered, some carelessly labelled, some go right back to my art-school days. All are crammed full to bursting with oddments of paper, photographs and bits of plants. When I pull one from the shelf, dry leaves and torn-off scraps tumble from it onto the floor, and I have to go down on my knees to gather them up again. The books are like a visual diary for me. I flick through the years as I leaf through their pages, in search of a passing thought that can be reharnessed, an image I half-remember. An idea that once got away.

The only untitled sketchbook opens in landscape, and there's a stained and ragged page ripped from a notebook stuck on the front. That was the year I spent making fantastical sundials for people's gardens. An exquisite little booklet falls out. It's hand-stitched with an azure-blue loose cover and a cream label printed by letterpress on rough card so you can feel the indents of each letter. The title is grand: *A Guide to Sundials with special reference to Portable Dials and Navigation Instruments including the work of Alex Monroe 1990–1992*. Tissue interleaves the pages, some of which are also printed by letterpress and some photocopied from sheets typed on an old-fashioned typewriter. In contrast, the sketchbook itself is a jumble of scribbled notes and drawings, all looking most scientific but almost unintelligible to me now. There are drawings of planets with angles described and mathematical symbols liberally scattered around. Every few pages I spot a little sketch of a classical column or some Byzantine jewellery. Long paragraphs have been written over in harsh black biro, the word WRONG scribbled several times.

Tucked into the inside back cover of *Yearbook 2000* is a wad of pressed tree leaves, mostly varieties of oak, all wrapped up in yellowing kitchen roll. I look at a carefully detailed, life-size sketch of an arum lily leaf – long spidery lines trace its veins – and some quick-fire studies showing the plant's cream-soft conical white flowers. I came across that bed of lilies in the far corner of a friend's garden in Kent. (I remember how sunny that June weekend turned out.) Elsewhere I see snowdrops in coloured pencil, pressed scarlet pimpernels, and notes on hydrangeas I've found in Greenwich Park and forget-me-nots on One Tree Hill. Finding another set of sketches labelled in Latin – *Saxifraga x urbium* – I remember how excited I was to discover London Pride in my own back garden, my pleasure in that pretty pink-freckled city fellow, full of frivolity and the indomitable spirit of the Blitz. I love its other common names too: Whimsey, Prattling Parnell, and my favourite, Look Up And Kiss Me. There's the start of a collection of jewellery just in that name.

In many ways these drawings are forensic. I'm gathering

information, clues as to how a thing works. Through drawing I can interpret and then reproduce the things I find. The other sketchbooks run chronologically. Sketchbook One starts when I was still at university, with a list of jobs to complete by 20 February 1985: *Finish hammers. Stamps. Start raising large bowl* . . . I made great big things back then – huge hand-raised bowls in patinated copper, formed by hammering great discs of metal for days on end. Having the tools and space and freedom made my ambitions large.

I'll do that again one day, I think. And turn the page.

Among a long series of clumsy drawings of patterns and bowls, I find a string of little hanging bottles, old terracotta ones. I have no memory of seeing or drawing them, but I realise it's the first sketch I've found that looks anything like jewellery. Then it all goes Celtic – a horse design deconstructed, some drinking vessels and a pattern of amusingly sad-looking fish. These I do remember. I drew them in the British Museum. *New Range*, it says triumphantly on the very last page of this book, above several drawings of a dead fish with a spear through it.

In Sketchbook Two I get into my stride. I'm a fully fledged jewellery designer now, and here are the pencil drawings to prove it. A year of cut fingers and frustration comes back to me with the sight of these designs for gold-foil-backed glass flower shapes with verdigris diving birds and carnelian beads. The attrition rate for these was high. I continue through pages of astrological designs to a mass of doodles of flowers and leaves, sketches from churches and hundreds of religious motifs and crosses. It's all very messy.

Sketchbook Three opens in 1997 with a series of designs for an American clothing company (*Fun, World Traveller, and Romantic Farm Girl*) and by Book Four I'm on very familiar territory. Little flowers on wreaths, and tiny insects. Pages and pages of butterfly wings, paisley swirls and leafy patterns and organic forms with scribbles and arrows and notes such as *Slightly Victorian sentimental* or *Umbel structure – see sputnik*. Pretty much wherever I have travelled and whatever I have done is recorded in a sketchbook somehow, even if it's just been scrawled on the back of an envelope and stuffed inside.

Perhaps this territory is getting too familiar. When something is working well, and buyers are calling for more, the biggest temptation is to give them more of the same. It's a problem for all designers after a while. It's so easy to become complacent. You've developed your signature style, it's going down a treat, and why would a leopard want to change his spots?

I remember a sign in the machine shop at art school: *Familiarity breeds contempt.*

If I don't want to go stale, it's time to scare myself. That should put life into the work. Starting work on The Gardener, I decide to have a go at something I feel really uncomfortable with. I'll approach this new collection in a completely different way. Before the jewellery, I'll create a story – an actual story – with a setting, a world of its own. A picture book. This will become an exhibition, and the jewellery will play its part.

My gardening obsession was seeded in the orchards of The Old Parsonage, among apples and apricots, pears and plums. Greengages were my favourites – there was something magical about their pale bloom, a powdery dullness, which you could polish away on your jumper, transforming the fruit into a shining gem. Sloes polished up well too, but they dried our mouths with sourness, and were best fed to a younger brother. Apples went on for months. The very first to crop was a small bright red fruit with a greasy skin, flesh stained pink, sweet as sugar, which fell from an unscalably tall tree quite early in August. The wasps liked them even more than I did. The very last to ripen was a russet we called Suffolk Spice. You could pick it right into November, up to Guy Fawkes Night. It was an easy climb to gather fruit with skin as matt as khaki emery paper, dry in the hand and rough on the tongue. It tasted of honey and cinnamon.

Each autumn the whole family turned out to pick apples to store in our cellars. We boys took great delight in scaring our sisters, who were waiting down below to catch the fruit we plucked. We shimmied along boughs as high and creaky as we could manage, always reaching for the fruit that seemed just out of our grasp. My father stretched out equally precariously from the top of a teetering stepladder. Then the seven of us turned into a production line, gently wrapping each apple in newspaper to stack in crates, while our hands turned black with newsprint. Well into the following spring, we'd still be eating the russets – soft-rough spongy bites of fermented spice.

Vegetables were a less communal affair. There was a greenhouse at The Old Parsonage but, like everything else, it was a wreck when we first arrived – the remains of a large structure with a steep roof pitched against a south-facing wall of high red brick. Behind the wall lurked a boiler-house. Cracked dry putty no longer did its job in the window frames, and every time the wind blew, more sheets of glass tumbled down and shattered. The peeling, rotten door was long off its hinges. Outside, the neglected vegetable beds and soft-fruit bushes had descended into jungle.

But in the spring of 1970 we got lucky. *Reader's Digest* was look-ing for a location to shoot a piece about restoring a dilapidated Victorian greenhouse. They needed a beautiful wreck to bring back to life. Could we oblige? The photographer was Michael Boys, a friend of my parents. I have a copy of the *Complete Do-It-Yourself Manual* in which our greenhouse featured. Thicker than two phone books, it's delightfully seventies in style, all browns and oranges with splashes of sombre greens. Stripped pine and white gloss; marigolds and ferns. It's a Margo and Jerry kind of Good Life, rather than Barbara and Tom's.

In the late 1960s, Michael had photographed *English Style* (Bodley Head, 1967), which remains one of my favourite reference books from that era. Terence Conran's cottage in Suffolk, along with many of his neighbours', illustrated the pared-down treatment of Victorian architecture that came into favour just then. It was a moment when nineteenth-century wrecks were the only affordable way many people could buy their own home. They were cold and drafty, with no central heating, and outside loos often enough. But they were also cheap and plentiful, and you could do what you liked with them. Designers like Conran offered inspiration for creative types who wanted to bring a bit of modernity into their new, old homes. Gone was all the clutter-clutter, carpets were chucked, floors and banisters were stripped, white paint was slapped straight onto unplastered brick walls. The odd piece of Victorian furniture was allowed alongside a modern minimalistic statement, in a confident mixture of below-stairs Victoriana and Twentieth-century Modern. People were hungry for manuals to show them how to achieve the New English look all by themselves. In 1972 the first DIY superstore opened in Britain: Texas Homecare.

How's the plot?

I was talking to one of the least likely allotment holders I know: a superbly glamorous young designer friend called Lesley, who is also a fashion photographer. It was nearly closing time for the show at Paris Fashion Week, and I'd wandered over to her stand for a bit of gossip. We ignored Buba's metallic-embroidered, fairy-tale handbags and discussed tomato blight instead.

Talking allotments and vegetable growing is a great antidote to all the showiness around us, though it's hard to give a conversation full attention when you're half-looking over each other's shoulders for approaching press or buyers. My own plot – which I share with a couple of friends – is a quiet refuge from that very public world of exhibiting and selling, a place for introverted reflection as much as cultivating plants. I told Lesley about the struggles I'd been having with the soil – it's tough getting a Suffolk-style tilth on London clay – and the fat, thieving squirrels, and also the record-breaking strawberry crop we'd had last year. She started telling me a touching tale about her daughter and a nice old chap they'd got to know at their allotment, and then our chat was cut short by a vibrating phone.

But something about Lesley's story lingered in the back of my mind long after we'd packed up Paris.

I couldn't remember the exact details, but that wasn't the point. I began to write my own version of her tale. A little girl and her mother are scrumping from an overhanging tree when they meet an old man on his allotment. He invites them in, chucking over his keys so they can unlock the gate. They enter a hidden world of raised beds and potting sheds. Cane pyramids of beans and delicious fruit. It's the beginning of a friendship, and soon the little girl and her mother are helping out regularly in the allotment. One day they visit the old man only to find he isn't there. Later they see his shed being cleared out and discover he has died. But he has left them a special gift: the bunch of keys. Now it's their turn to look after the allotment.

The story needed illustrating so I asked an old friend, Katharine Nicholls, to try a few watercolours. Swirling circles of greens, blues and browns in a dreamy summertime haze. Perfect.

I also needed a place where I could recreate the story's setting. A potting shed full of plants and tools and tiny watering cans right in the centre of town. Penhaligon's, the perfumiers, had just the right space at the back of their Covent Garden shop. A phone call to another old friend, Emily, and a plan was made and a date set. We could have the room from Friday 10 July for a couple of weeks. Friday would be press day. We used one of Kathy's illustrations for the invitations and sent them out. There, it was done. No going back. I had two months to get this done. And I hadn't even begun to design the jewellery.

But already I knew I wanted to display it in a living setting, silver and gold appearing magically among real growing plants, arranged on moss and twigs and grass. Back in my workshop at home I built a series of oversized seed trays out of old timber, salvaged long ago for just this sort of eventuality. I headed out to the countryside to forage. Tiny nettles and holly seedlings from Suffolk; mossy rocks and ferns from Wales. Hazel branches from the woods down near Pin Mill to cut into minute logs. I planted up my seed trays and scattered grass seed over the bare patches. Now they just needed to grow, and for the plants to spread and intertwine. This was going to take a great deal of care and patience.

Meanwhile, Kathy and I put the finishing touches to the book, and by that time the jewellery was almost designing itself. I drew sketches for a bunch of keys, plant labels, some rough garden string and a smooth apple. There was a bee buzzing by and a pea ready to pick. A tiny watering can with a drip just hanging from its spout. But time was running out and each piece still had to be made.

Thanks to *Reader's Digest,* The Old Parsonage greenhouse was miraculously restored. A wide brick path running down its length was revealed, leading you from the half-glazed gloss-white wooden door, which now opened without a struggle. The dusty red brickwork still looked deliciously aged, but new slatted wooden workbenches now rose above a suitably Victorian fern bed. The place smelled of paint, putty and pine. And it felt big.

If we'd stoked up the still-working stove in the boiler-house on the other side of the wall, we could have grown almost anything in there. Pineapples or peaches – all kinds of exotic glories. But we stuck with the basics: tomatoes in the greenhouse, and salad in the cold frames that stood just outside. Out in the wide beds of the garden beyond grew all the standard veg: carrots, potatoes, courgettes and spinachey sorts of greens. There was no talk of heritage varieties in those days. This was simply food production. Growing to eat was as important to our survival as the chickens and ducks that roamed the orchards and tried to hide their eggs. When the garden went well, we ate lots. When it didn't, we ate less.

Leftovers were precious, fed to the poultry or scraped into a huge cast-iron pot, which constantly simmered on the warm-plate of the Aga, a perpetually evolving soup stock.

Nikki was cook, although she rarely sat down to eat with us. She would start the day at dawn, bringing mugs of hot sweet tea to our rooms, and end it by thumping a saucepan of vegetable stew onto the table and storming off, complaining that she couldn't work wonders and how could she feed a family if there was no food in the cupboards.

I took over the running of the greenhouse during my last term at primary school and was quickly caught up in the magic of making things grow. I learned how to germinate seeds in trays and persuade cuttings to take root, how to transplant seedlings and dispatch snails. I gathered together the right tools for each job – dibbers and daisy-grubbers; mattocks and hand hoes – but I only needed my fingers for my favourite task, which was pinching out the side shoots from the tomato plants, releasing an unmistakable tomatoey smell. Later came the reward of popping a warm ripe fruit into my mouth, and bursting it between my teeth.

That summer I had plenty of time to experiment. Term started late at the public school in Ipswich, where I'd won a scholarship as a day boy. Even early in the autumn, I could get back from school just before the light faded. I remember a noticeable chill in the air outside, but in my greenhouse, the bricks were still warm. I'd come in and inhale the clean rich smell of tomato leaves and geraniums and damp soil, then head straight over to an upturned terracotta flowerpot. There was a pile of them in one corner, which could have been care-lessly – exquisitely – arranged for a photoshoot. My hand would reach underneath and pull out my stash of cigarette packets, bought from anonymous Ipswich vending machines with our home-made fifty-pence pieces. Another pot hid my matches. I lit up and began to puff away on a Players No. 6, Finest Virginia. For an eleven-year-old boy, this really was the Good Life. I had claimed the first bit of my own territory.

Bees I know; I've made bees before. The countless hours spent at my bench carving the bee for my Original Sin collection have lodged in my fingertips. This one is different of course, bumbling around, tipsy on pollen, wings in mid-flight, but the techniques are much the same. Keys, too, are straightforward, and anyway, I have a huge collection of old locks and keys at home. But the pea . . . how does a pea work? Luckily I grow them on the allotment, so it's easy enough to find out.

My plot's not far away and the timing's right, so I jump on my bike and race off right away, up and down a few hills, to see how they're coming along. Our allotment is very picturesque. Squeezed between the South Circular and Dulwich Woods, near a cricket club and a tennis club, part of it nestles under a huge willow tree. But that makes it shady, and what with the London clay, which floods in the winter and cracks up like concrete in the summer, not to mention the couch grass and the snails and the pigeons, it often feels a losing battle. For me, though, that isn't the point. It's still a place where I can escape for a few hours a week. I never expected to tame it, but I've enjoyed having a go.

There are a few different types of pea: fatter ones for shelling, and the flatter mangetout varieties, which we've been growing, though they're looking a bit ragged as they clamber over green netting and twiggy hazel sticks. I pick several good ones – slightly overripe, calyx as jaunty as a pixie hat. I look around and feel tempted to stay here longer. The plot badly needs watering, and the weeds are fighting for space with the onions. Turning my back on it all, I sling my rucksack on my shoulder and set off for the studio, calculating as I pedal exactly how many days there are left before 10 July.

Dissecting the peas back at the workbench, I try to work out precisely what it is I like so much about them. They are very tactile. They have a matt bloom on their skins that reminds me of those childhood greengages, and you can rub them between finger and thumb to make them shine up just as beautifully. There is a satisfying contrast between the smooth curve of the pod and the spiky calyx and stalk. But most appealing thing of all is the peas-in-the-pod element. It's an idea and a reality: the undulating belly of the fruit holding its sugar-sweet seeds.

Popping the first one open I can see how it was made. Firstly there's the stem. Its circle of sepals once enclosed the blossom and now they hold on to the fruit. The fruit itself has two layers of skin,

The Gardner + write the story.

"The present" + keyring   The fish   the key

Pods etc

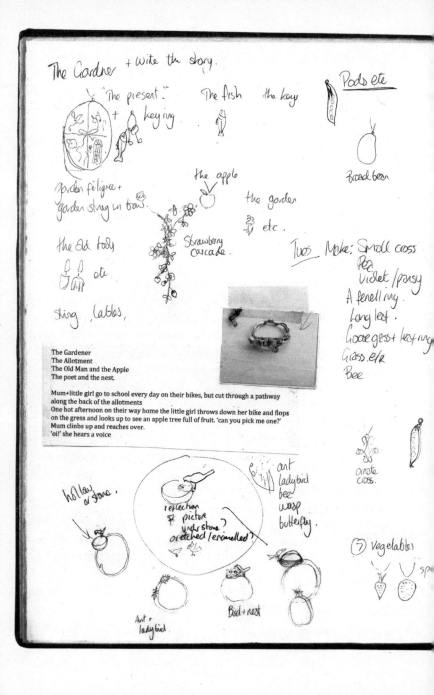

Broad bean

garden filigree +
garden string in bow.

the apple

the garden
etc.

the old tools
etc.

Strawberry cascade.

Tuos Make: Small cross
Pea
violet / pansy
A fennel ring.
Long leaf.
Gooegess + leaf ring
Grass. e/r
Bee

string, cables,

The Gardener
The Allotment
The Old Man and the Apple
The poet and the nest.

Mum+little girl go to school every day on their bikes, but cut through a pathway
along the back of the allotments
One hot afternoon on their way home the little girl throws down her bike and flops
on the gress and looks up to see an apple tree full of fruit. 'can you pick me one?'
Mum clinbs up and reaches over.
'oi!' she hears a voice

hollow
or stone.

reflection
& picture
under stone?
or etched / enamelled?

ant
ladybird
bee
wasp
butterfly.

onote cross.

Ant +
ladybird.

Bird + nest

(7) Vegetables

ladybug studs
butterfly studs
wood bee studs

snail studs.
bird on chain.

wood bee

Penhaligons

ants with tiny pins to fix things.

ants on honey stone

leaping dragonfly

smaller bee

ants x 100 ! + Red ants.

½ chain ½ bangle the "brangle"

woven straw ring

also with dia?

ants on ring x100's

crown bottle top. (mini?) with writing

twisty straw ring.

Rolled up. grass.

this area is key.

Grass E/R

slightly smoother uppa

ant with leaf

grass, chain + string bangle?

Make it with
{ 3.
{ cast, cut out
{ ?

Box piece

Mini Bamboo!

New beginnings. The future

String + blossom

watering can.

Ant lady bird.

What about these little fellows?
floaty

Can I source very thin silver chain!

and a kind of frame, to which the little peas are attached. The outer form is created as the peas within gradually swell. The only way I can reproduce that is by doing exactly the same, but in miniature.

I cut six tiny discs from a sheet of silver. They vary in size, but all are between 2mm and 3mm – almost too small to hold. These will be my peas, and I need to find a way to file them into spheres. On my last trip to Japan I bought a pair of pliers so fine I wasn't sure what I would use them for. Here's my chance to try them out. Optivisors on, I pinch the largest disc in the pliers and start to file. Ten minutes later, six peas in a row sit in front of me.

The frame has to be a hair's width thin. After drawing and redrawing I settle on a shape, reduce it down to about 25mm and transfer the drawing onto a sheet of wafer-thin silver. Cutting it out is a precarious business. The silver is so fine it can't support its own weight, far less tolerate any slipping or snagging with the piercing saw: if its shape is distorted in the slightest, the piece will be ruined. I find myself holding my breath. Along the inside curve of the frame I leave six little teeth. I'll be soldering the peas to these. And then I cut out the skins a second time, again in a sheet thinner than tracing paper. Lastly the calyx. This I cut in two halves without the stalk attached. I will solder on a short section of wire later.

I gently lie out the pea-pod-shaped frame on a charcoal block and arrange the miniature peas inside, from small to large to small again. It looks odd when I've soldered each one into place, like an X-ray of a pea-pod. Next I make a sandwich, layering the two flat skins on either side of my skeleton and tacking them into place with the tiniest speck of solder. I'm hoping that if I squish the two skins together in a rolling mill, they will gently take the shape of the peas inside, giving the lovely undulating fat-belly curves of the pea. Texture is important too. I want to reproduce the soft bloom you just can't help wanting to touch. I sandwich layers of rough cartridge paper on either side of my pea-pod and bind the whole thing up in masking tape. Now for the squishing.

My rolling mills work something like a mangle. Turn a long crank and the two steel rollers turn. The height of the rollers can be adjusted by turning a screw on the top. I adjust it to what I think is about right and start turning the crank, feeding my paper parcel into the rollers as I turn. It catches and pulls the parcel in. The crank stiffens – too tight? I use two hands and pull with all my might. Half a turn more and the squished-flat parcel plops out on the other side.

That ought to do it.

The masking tape and paper have been destroyed, so it's hard to peel away the wrapping from my little silver pea. It's like opening a Christmas present. I scratch and tear over-eagerly, stickiness collecting under my nails, and suddenly there it is, a tiny little pea-pod, softly bulging with promise. It's worked.

No time to linger: this is exciting. It needs the touch of a file where the two sides don't quite meet precisely enough. There. Then I plop it back on the forge and solder up the joins. I have to bend the calyx halves slightly to make them fit, solder them on, then there's just the right little curve of wire which makes the stem. Into the pickle, a minute or two in the barrel polisher and I'm ready to show the others in the workshop. After a huddle of coos, I know I'm on track. This pea is going to be all right. In fact I know the whole collection is going to work now. I just need to crack on and get it all made.

My anxiety grows as press day approaches: *The Gardener, an exhibition and story to introduce a new collection of jewellery at Penhaligon's in Covent Garden.* It sounds almost as grand as my thesis on sundials. The concept of writing a story and putting on an exhibition to launch a collection out of season takes some explaining in the fashion world. And I know that it will only really work if we can muster a bit of enchantment on the day. But the press are interested. Emma has done her work well. The invitations have all been sent and we have a long list of RSVPs, and some wonderful goodie-bags for attendees. Editors and writers have been phoning up for a sneak preview but Emma is suitably mysterious.

You'll just have to come and see for yourself.

★

It looks like the Hanging Gardens of Babylon on wheels. The roof rack of my car is alarmingly laden with overgrown seed trays and trailing greenery. I'm struggling to see anything in my rear-view mirror other than the display equipment packed inside: lights and tables and chairs and boxes filled with catalogues and brochures. It's press-launch day and I pull up outside Penhaligon's at eight in the morning to find that Richard, the shop manager, isn't there yet. Emma and Susie Lee and I unload, and I leave them guarding the piles on the pavement while I set off to find a parking place. By the time I'm back, the shop door is open and everyone is shifting boxes and bags inside.

Two *By Appointment* signs above the door add to the reassuringly old-fashioned appearance bestowed by Penhaligon's polished-brass-and-plum frontage. The Covent Garden shop on Wellington Street sits between the London Transport Museum and the London Film Museum, and today there are bunches of pink balloons fluttering from the awning. Inside, it looks dark and mysterious and, as you walk in, an enticing mishmash of perfumes floods your nostrils. It's an Aladdin's cave for the senses. I once had an evening out on the town with the perfumier from Penhaligon's, and I'm reminded of it now: it was an intriguing visit to a world experienced purely through smell.

A great circular table covered in glass tester pots stands in the middle of the shop. The walls around are lined with dark wooden cabinets full of coloured bottles and boxes lit by a thousand twinkling lights. There are several old sets of drawers that wouldn't look out of place in an apothecary's shop, and a vast Victorian shaving sink in porcelain and chrome. The fireplace has already been lavishly decorated in a cottage garden theme.

In these dimly lit surroundings, Richard now stands and glows, his primrose-yellow trousers and pink waistcoat beaming at me like a burst of sunshine on a grey day. He welcomes in all our old gardening tools and bamboo canes, our piles of hand-thrown clay pots and galvanised-tin watering cans. We begin to set up the exhibition. The idea is to

114

recreate the feel of an archetypal potting shed or greenhouse. We arrange two faded canvas garden chairs beside a rickety old table strewn with vintage gardening magazines and make sure there's a pile of my picture books ready to be picked up as you come in. Plants sprout and tumble from a two-metre-long wooden seed tray of moss and grass along the back wall. In the centre of the room stand three stacks of old fruit boxes, each topped with a seed tray planted with all sorts of weeds, lit by miniature spotlights. An earthy smell is beginning to mingle with the perfumes. It's all ready now for me to lay out the jewellery.

The first to arrive is the gang from *Marie Claire*. Old friends, so I enjoy taking them round and explaining everything. It helps get me into my stride for I can't help responding to their delight. More people arrive before long and then the day swims by. In the afternoon Emilia Fox pops in. I take her out for a late lunch and as we sit in the restaurant I can see people stealing looks at us. I'm lunching with a beautiful actress and at last I can believe this exhibition is going to be a success. For once I stop worrying about what is coming next and enjoy the moment.

Then I show Emilia round the exhibition, and she loves it. Every seed tray is a tiny landscape, an inviting green world carefully planned to look perfectly wild and natural. Small logs are half-buried, with tiny tendrils of ivy climbing over them as if they have lain untouched and rotting for years. Grass grows between rocks and mossy bricks. My lifelong habit of collecting dead insects and mollusc shells has come in handy. Snails and beetles lurk in crevices. A little daisy is just opening up its petals and minute stinging nettles emerge here and there, the tiny hairs on their leaves softly catching the light. I've placed each piece of jewellery on a rock or a tiny fallen tree trunk, where they sparkle under the pinpoint spotlights, gleaming beautifully. The pea-pod earrings look perfect on the cut surface of an upturned log. I adjust the lights slightly to catch the sapphire waterdrop of the tiny watering can shimmering beside them. Emilia picks out her favourite pieces. Someone takes a photograph.

*

In winter at The Old Parsonage, when the greenhouse became too cold even for me, I had another retreat. I spent much of my four-teenth year in the enclosed red-lit world of my darkroom, discovering the possibilities offered by photographic paper and plant forms. It was no more than a windowless broom-cupboard really, halfway down the long corridor running between my parents' room and the girls' quarters. I'd installed a worktop, and I had a projector, which I could swing over the edge and project onto the floor if I needed to, for something really big. Then there were the usual developing tanks and fixing tanks and a red lamp, clipped to a shelf.

I could only develop and print black-and-white film, but I also loved making photograms.

Even then I was drawn to natural forms. I laid translucent flowers and leaves on photographic paper, experimenting with different arrangements of grasses and ferns – unfurling fiddle heads, patterns of spores, spikelets of fescue flower. Playing around with spiky umbellifer heads or stag-beetle antlers, I shaded some areas, over-exposed others, and finally I would expose the whole thing to light. The next stage was to dip the prints in trays of developer, then watch and wait with narrowed eyes peering through the red half-light, until the image magically appeared. Out with the tweezers. A quick dunk in a bucket of water, and then into the fixative. After a final rinse, I could peg each print onto a little washing line before turning on the main light to see the results.

When I was younger I used to collect pillowcases of chestnuts to sell to a neighbour for his pigs, or to eat at home. In late November one year I thought of putting their husks to a new purpose, in my photography experiments. It was a close call whether to have a go at that, or to develop some images of ferns viewed from inside the greenhouse, or begin to explore the possibilities of my ever-growing feather collection. But our most recent autumnal scavengings had produced a good variety of conker shells and beechnuts and chestnut husks, so I decided to try out different combinations on photo-graphic paper. I had reached the fiddling around stage. A group here . . . or would this look better over here? I stood back to get some perspective and caught my hand on the wire from the light. It unclipped itself from the shelf and plopped sizzling into the bucket of water, plunging me instantly into darkness.

I fumbled for the doorknob and felt my way out into the dim corridor, where I hesitated, unsure of my next move. Far away downstairs, my parents were hosting a party. Now that I was out of the darkroom, I could just hear the odd wave of laughter, building and dying like distant surf. I could picture all those tipsy grown-ups with their intrusive questions, boozy hugs and lipstick-smudged kisses. The last thing I wanted to do was draw attention to myself. Anyway, children were absolutely banned from the drawing room. We had a firm understanding about this: children could do whatever they wanted, anywhere in the house, as long as they didn't disturb the grown-ups in the drawing room. The grown-ups, in turn, could do whatever they wanted there, I suppose.

But I had a feeling I ought to seek some advice. I set off in the direction of the party, and paused before knocking on the big white door at the foot of the front stairs. Behind me the vast hall stood

My parents looking very glamorous at an evening do.

empty, grand piano and music-stands in one corner, a colossal square column in the centre of the room, lifeless fire-places opening up on either side of it.

No reply. I could hear loud music, so they probably hadn't heard me. I turned the cold white porcelain door handle and pushed the heavy door open. The room was full of grown-ups, lounging and laughing in three great sagging sofas round the

117

hearth, or standing around on colourful Casa Pupo rugs – they came from Spain, via Pimlico, and looked impressively continental scattered over wooden floorboards. Other guests were propped against swirling grey-patterned wallpaper, or supported themselves with an outstretched arm against one of the floor-to-ceiling bookcases, leaning into some intimate conversation or shared joke. A few more perched on the ornate club fender, their cheeks glowing from a blazing fire. Through whisky-scented smoke, and noisy, whirling, classical dance music – Hungarian rhapsodies perhaps, or Berlioz, or Liszt? – I peered around, trying to locate my father. Twisting towards him between the guests, I quietly told him what had happened. How the light had fallen in the water.

Well, take it out! he said, as though it were the most obvious thing in the world. *But don't forget to unplug it from the wall first.*

Darling, darling, oh do come over here . . . a grown-up was calling to me. A woman across the room in silk and *décolleté*, beckoning me over. Quick! I darted out and back up the long staircase, out of the bright, noisy drawing-room bustle and into the quiet grey and dark green of the unlit staircase. Up to the landing, right, then left along the corridor, and I was back at my darkroom, now pitch black. Hurry, hurry. How would I ever find the light? I fumbled about for it, starting at the plug and following the flex down and into the bucket, which I could just see now that my eyes were beginning to adjust to the darkness. I reached into the murky water and grabbed it.

Every muscle in my body seemed to contract instantly. I was knocked right out of the room and into the hallway. Still standing, I juddered about like a cartoon character, my hand locked onto the light with a terrible force. I had never known pain like this; I didn't know if I could bear its intensity, ever-growing, constricting everything with a frightening purity. My body was completely rigid yet I twitched uncontrollably as I danced my solo electric rhapsody. My brain still seemed to be working, which meant that a detached part of me could watch as smoke started to rise from my hand. The light at the far end of the hall flickered as I sapped its power. And soon a dark cloud began to fog my vision. The pain grew even stronger, creeping along my arm and into my torso and I vaguely registered the fact that I must be losing consciousness.

In the drawing room downstairs, the party swung on until one or two guests remarked on the flickering lights. One by one they stopped talking and the room fell silent. Deprived of current, the record player ran unevenly, slowing down and speeding up, grotesquely distorting the music, until it sounded like the soundtrack to a scene from a horror movie.

Darling, perhaps you should see what's going on . . . Peggy-Ann sent Stuart to investigate, and a couple of other sturdy chaps came too.

I must have just about hung onto consciousness until they found me, or maybe they revived me, for I remember being rather annoyed as they started to hit me with a broom. I gather the plan was to hit the light out of my hand with the broom handle. Luckily someone had the sense to pull the flex out of the wall. I fell in a crumpled heap on the floor, smoke still rising from my hand and arm, giving off an unpleasant smell of cooking flesh.

But I wasn't dead, simply knocked out for a while. I was carried to my bed and, as usual, my sisters were fetched. They cleaned up my hand and wrapped it in bandages made from torn-up old sheets. With the power supply fully restored, the party swung on. I woke to a familiar smell of Dettol and zinc and castor-oil cream.

For the Gardener display at London Fashion Week, I had photographed and printed out a muted panorama of my allotment in Dulwich to dress the back panels of the stand. The rest of the display was to be taken directly from the exhibition, which I had taken down two months previously. The same quirky potting shed set-up with crates and seed trays. The gardening magazines. The stacked flowerpots in red clay. The old garden chairs. There was a slight problem of fitting everything in this time.

The grand white plasterwork and wooden floors of Somerset

House would have made the perfect backdrop for our elegant English garden in muted pastel colours. It was looking distinctly out of place in this industrial setting but Emma and Suzy remained optimistic, and my hopes rose too. Until I stepped back to survey our work and tripped on that odd bit of stand-frame which was still sticking out. We had asked repeatedly to get it removed so I thought I might as well do the job myself. It surely wouldn't take a minute. I was unscrewing the crucial nut when someone booted me gently in the backside and said: *What the fuck do you think you're doing?*

A workman was staring down at me in indignant disbelief. A brief period of chaos followed, and workmates and health and safety supervisors were summoned. However I explained myself, I managed to rub them all up the wrong way. The workman got more and more heated. The others kept shouting *Health and Safety* at me and I tried to explain that was exactly why I wanted it moved. But there was no way out for me. The men were getting really angry. I stopped what I was doing and apologised. Soon the small crowd dispersed.

But I had a plan. I asked Emma and Suzy to hold up a tablecloth as you would if you wanted to change into your trunks on a beach. Only I wasn't going to change into my trunks: I was going to unbolt that bloody strut at last. They were unhappy with my plan but I soon persuaded them. Two minutes later the job was done. Easy. Or it would have been if I hadn't noticed another stray strut sticking out at just over 6 foot. Now that I had spotted it, I really wanted it gone too. The problem was that I needed a stepladder. The place was still teeming with workmen and there were lots of stepladders dotted around. It would only take two seconds. Nearby I found an unattended ladder and whisked it away.

If I do this quickly nobody will notice.

Emma and Suzy weren't so sure. I nipped up, whisked out my Allen key and started unscrewing the strut when suddenly the stepladder shook beneath me and I nearly toppled off. I grabbed the top of my stand and I looked down, half-hanging, to see the same furious workman pulling the ladder out from underneath me. He was shouting. Emma and Suzy were shouting. Soon a considerably larger crowd gathered. It seemed to egg me on.

Why don't you just fuck off and leave me alone? I said.

The workman's fists were already clenched and he pounced first and tried to throw a punch. Emma and Suzy and several bystanders jumped in to stop him and I was bundled off down the narrow spiral staircase. Outside I sat and fumed. Then I stood up and paced angrily. And when Emma reappeared, I snapped.

Enough is enough, I said. *We're leaving. Break down the show and see how they like that.*

Emma looked me hard in the eyes as you might stare down a small child. More firmly than ever, she told me to bugger off. And don't come back. So I did. And I didn't. That was the last time I was allowed anywhere near London Fashion Week.

Daisy Bell

Today I'm meeting Roddy for lunch. We meet every week in the same place, the Anchor and Hope in Waterloo. Locked to a tree outside is a 1980s tangerine Bianchi, my weekday commuting bicycle. One of an ever-increasing collection, it's a beautiful bike, with sweeping Nitto handlebars in the shape of Conan Doyle-style whiskers. I bought them in Tokyo to fit to a frame imported from San Francisco. Roddy is chatting away when I look up from my potted shrimps to see three or four people standing round it. One man squats down and examines more closely. I don't even say anything to Roddy. I just glance over at them quickly, feel like a million bucks and smile a secret smile to myself.

There is something special about the freedom a bicycle gives you. When I was nine or ten it was a step-through Raleigh Jeep. Freewheeling down the road to the marina with the wind in my face, I was half-intoxicated, half-terrified. Now my most treasured possession is a hand-built Roberts, made for me like a bespoke suit by Chas Roberts, the finest frame builder in the south. I did the aesthetics; Chas did the technical stuff. It's that perfect marriage of form and function again, the work of a real craftsman. I've cycled the thousand miles from Land's End to John O'Groats on my Roberts, on the greatest adventure in British cycling. Just you and your bike and the open road.

You never forget your first bike, though. Not long ago I found a Raleigh Jeep on eBay and bought it for my daughter. It wasn't in too bad a shape, arriving flat-packed in a ropey old cardboard box. The handlebars were at ninety degrees, the pedals had been removed, and everything rattled like crazy. It needed new brakes and cables, of course, and I could only find those unusual size tyres online. But a tin of oil and a couple of hours in my workshop later, it was as good as new. Orange-red frame, metallic blue mudguards and a slip-stream chain guard. Three Sturmey Archer gears. Whitewalled wheels to match the saddle and handlebar grips. A bike to be proud of and beautiful to ride, it has an old-fashioned long wheel-base with forks that stretch lazily forwards so it almost steers itself. Connie loves it as much as I loved mine.

In Suffolk she glides along the back lanes and freewheels down towards Iken Church, with me keeping a safe distance behind. I want to give her the independence I enjoyed in my youth and I don't want to break in on the fun, but still I can't bear to miss out on seeing her enjoy it. Connie is twelve and she can feel the wind in her face. I remember that feeling all too well and I want to capture it somehow in my next collection. Freedom. Being on the brink of something exciting, something you can sense, although you don't yet know quite what it is. Freewheeling down through the dappled shade.

That Raleigh Jeep is my starting point. I trace its outline in fine pencil in my sketchbook, and I'm reminded of a song. So under the sketch I write:

> *Daisy, Daisy, give me your answer do,*
> *I'm half crazy, all for the love of you.*
> *It won't be a stylish marriage, I can't afford a carriage.*
> *But you'll look sweet upon the seat of a bicycle built for two.*

There is something about that song that I can't get out of my head.

There is a flower within my heart . . .
Planted one day by a glancing dart.

He's begging her to marry him.

You'll be the bell which I'll ring, you know
Sweet little Daisy Bell
You'll take the lead on each trip we'll take
Then if I don't do well
I'll permit you to use the brake . . .

It's about setting off on a journey through life together. But it's also about sex. I imagine the scene: a picnic, a young couple – pretty, handsome – cycling out into the countryside on a beautiful sunny day. Warm from the exercise, they find a secluded spot in the shade under a vast oak tree and lay out a blanket. It's lunchtime. They laugh and they joke, feeling carefree and uninhibited. She is lying on her back, sunlight speckled on her pale white face. Soft pink lips. She covers her mouth with a hand as she bursts into laughter and he rolls over in play fight and she squeals with delight. But suddenly they stop. They look at one another and see something in each other's eyes. Their laughter turns into smiles, serious smiles, and as he leans down, she raises her chin and lifts her head. They kiss a kiss as long and warm as the summer's day. And then I notice something off to one side. Some rather bold mice are taking advantage of the situation, rummaging around in the picnic basket, looking for cake and chocolate. A glass has toppled over and spilled its wine.

My daydream has quickly turned into a cliché from a romantic film but I don't care. A well-used image can often make a good starting point. It offers the kernel of an idea that you know will be both familiar and appealing, with instant resonance, but there's always scope for development: a good dollop of reality and a twist of your own. I make a few notes in my sketchbook, hastily pencilling a wicker picnic basket with the mouse inside and a bottle of wine and an overturned glass.

For me it wasn't Daisy. It was Sally Beaumont and she wasn't a cliché. She was real and she was the flower within my heart.

As far as I was concerned, there was simply no argument. Sally Beaumont was the most gorgeous girl in the whole of East Anglia. She was a little bit punky, in a schoolgirl sort of a way, with a blonde bob, soft pale downy skin and a full figure, pink-and-orange punkette make-up, big eyes and a wide mouth. Her plump pale-pink lips parted when she smiled, revealing the whitest teeth I ever saw. In the summer of 1979 she was probably about sixteen. I couldn't believe that anyone so beautiful could exist in the world.

I knew her through my friend Jaki, who was all you could ever want in a best mate. We laughed, we argued, we messed about and it was fantastically uncomplicated, despite the fact that Roddy had recently fallen for her romantically, successfully wooing her away from another boyfriend. Sally was her best friend, so the four of us became a bit of a gang: Jaki, Sally and I all about the same age and Roddy just a couple of years older.

One morning, late in the long summer holidays, the two girls and I were hanging around in the walled garden, soaking up the sun, finishing our tea and toast. Roddy had already disappeared, setting off early to get to work on a boat he'd just bought with another friend. *Victoria* was a small cutter, built at the end of the nineteenth century to patrol the valuable oyster beds on the river Colne. She was berthed at Bourne Bridge on the Wherstead road, where the Orwell meets the outskirts of Ipswich.

Sally wanted to see the boat but Jaki had to get back to town so I offered to take Sally down to the moorings myself. We could walk along the river. It was only five or six miles to the bridge.

We packed a small picnic, grabbed a couple of bikes from the barn and pushed them up through the garden. Along by the old garages, round the kitchen gardens and greenhouse, we followed future ideas: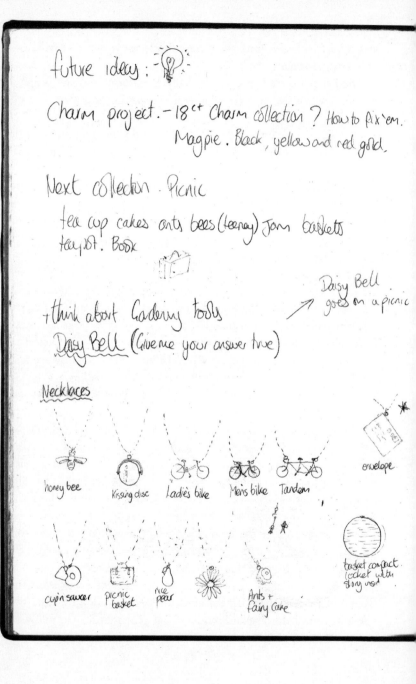

Charm project. - 18ct Charm collection ? How to fix 'em.
                    Magpie. Black, yellow and red gold.

Next collection. Picnic
    tea cup cakes ants bees (teeny) Jam baskets
    teapot. Book

                                                    Daisy Bell.
                                            → goes on a picnic
+ think about Gardening tools
Daisy Bell (Give me your answer true)

Necklaces

honey bee   Kissing disc   Ladies bike   Mens bike   Tandem   envelope

cup in saucer   picnic   rice   [flower]   Ants +   basket compact.
                 basket   pear   Fairy cake   locket with
                                                                  story inside

Daisy Bell

Daisy, Daisy
Give me your answer do!
I'm half crazy
All for the love of you
It won't be a stylish marriage
I can't afford a marriage
But you'll look sweet upon the seat
of a bicycle built for two

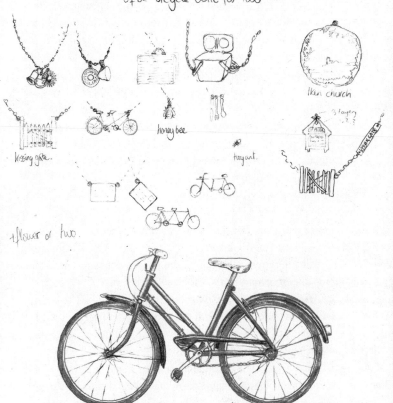

Iken church

kissing gate.

honey bee

tiny ant.

+ flower or two.

the high red-brick wall with its soft, rounded coping stones, from which we used to launch ourselves onto the Tarzan rope. Past Top Field and through the Japanese knotweed jungle. Down the long, shady path, once thick with mantraps. And then we burst out through the old wooden gate into bright open parkland and the smell of sun on grass. As we walked through the shade of a huge sweet chestnut tree, the air grew cool and I noticed goosebumps on Sally's arms.

Back in the open, swallows swooped down with incredible speed and agility, nearly brushing the grass with their wingtips before darting back up again. What could possibly be better than that? Except this: I had Sally Beaumont to myself and I could feel the sun on the back of my neck.

On the white concrete of the marina road, we hopped onto our bikes and freewheeled down the long straight hill. Stacks of huge polystyrene blocks, each the size of a car, stood around, waiting to be made into pontoons for the new marina. A few days earlier I'd watched the Airfix glue I'd poured into one block burn right through the polystyrene like acid. Now I was watching Sally's face, lit up and thrilled by the speed of our downhill coast. She grinned her widest smile, and so did I and we whooped.

Just before the sharp bend by the Cat House we turned off, pedalling hard to make it up the last few yards of the steep slope towards the tuck shop. We propped our bikes against the shop's larch-lap cladding. Sally was intrigued as I led her down a set of giant concrete steps, moulded like so many bars of chocolate, and plummeting down into the darkness of a steep wooded slope. We used to skid down the muddy slide here on dustbin lids. I was beyond that now. I took Sally's hand in mine and helped her down the first massive step.

Oh my God! Where are you taking me?

At the bottom we found the path through the trees that ran parallel to the river. Here the air was cool and damp, the feral rhododendrons well past flowering. Spots of sunlight dappled their dark shiny leaves, and the soft spiking mares' tails gave the place a prehistoric feel.

Greens and browns and a soft mossy carpet. The steep earthen slope rising above us on our left was thick with tall trees, ferns and fallen logs. On our right, bright sunshine caught the river. There was an occasional sharp birdcall. Pigeons clapped their wings in flight. We didn't talk much.

After a few hundred yards the path became difficult, so I found a good place to climb down to the water's edge. There was a fallen tree trunk, like a bridge from the bank. Holding on to a branch, I scrambled down and held out my hand again for Sally. She jumped down to me. I was standing on a soft mass of twigs and seaweed at the top of the tide-line. She flicked her hair off her face and smiled again.

We walked along the soft sand. The tide was going out and there was no danger of getting cut off. Up ahead, I could see where the shore widened further. It was sunnier there, with tree branches dipping onto the muddy sand, reedy, weedy flotsam caught up in their twigs. I noticed the skeleton of a dead seabird, washed up by the river and bleached white, but for once, I didn't pick it up.

Away from the bewitching shadows of the undergrowth, we both seemed to open up. We began to chat freely and we laughed. Sally took off her shoes and tucked her skirt up into her knickers so she could splash in the water. Birds sang in the trees on our left and somewhere out on the river, I could hear the distant drone of an outboard motor. Every so often we came to a tree which had fallen out into the river, stretching out seaweed-clad branches. We clambered over the trunks, pausing sometimes to sit on top, chatting or simply taking in the beauty of it all, admiring the intensity of the sunlight on the other side of the river. And then we would jump off with a crunch on the sandy shingle and run off chasing one another.

Past alder and willow oak and a vast ash, just clinging on to the bank. From time to time the gargled screech of a black-headed gull tried to interrupt our now unstoppable conversation. We had to leap over a little stream gushing out from the bank. The water ran through the woods from Freston village, smelling of freshly crushed leaves.

After Si Blackwell's house, the shore grew cleaner. The bank on our left levelled out, while the river opened up and curved off to our right. Then we reached a tall pine tree and a thicket of silver birches.

The road used to run along the shore here. A long time ago, of course. One terrible stormy night a coach crashed, killing all inside. And to this day on a dark night you can hear horses galloping, a terrifying crash and the screams of a dying woman.

Have you heard it?

I had to shake my head.

But I can show you the gravestone if you like.

Her lips parted and she nodded, so up we climbed, Sally still barefoot. Just as I remembered, a large granite stone was hidden in the undergrowth. I pushed aside the long wet grass and read the inscription aloud, in a doom-laden voice.

This stone marks the spot on which a four-wheel carriage was accidentally overturned on 31 July 1893. All the four occupants were mercifully saved.

My voice tailed off.

What? Mercifully saved? What's the bloody point of that?

Sally shrieked with laughter and took the piss. *Ooo . . . look out, the ghosts are coming to get you . . .*

She turned and ran back down to the river and I chased her. Back on the shore Sally raced ahead. Tripping as I went, I pulled off my canvas deck shoes and ran barefoot after her. We were right on the apex of the river's curve. We ran out into the shallow water and Sally turned and kicked splashes at me. The scene is fixed in my mind for ever, Sally giggling in white cheesecloth, the sun sparkling on water droplets, caught in a warm wind. Life in slow motion. I splashed her in turn and we then ran back though water and silky-warm mud which squidged between our toes, then soft brown sand, a strip of sharp shingle and finally onto the bank where the grass rolls gently up towards Freston Tower. There was the odd spiky thistle and dandelion but the ground was soft and warm. Sally flopped down to lie on her back. The grass was lush, heated by the sun, deeper than an eiderdown. I lay beside her and we both looked up at the sky. A huge Constable sky with puffy white clouds. The wind swished in the trees behind us and in the distance sounded the plaintive cry of a sandpiper.

Sally's white blouse was slightly translucent and damp in places. I could see the shape of her breasts, and her stomach rising as she breathed. The fine downy hair on her arms shone in the sun. She wore a silver bangle and a thong of dark leather casually tied around her wrist and as she moved her arms they slid softly along her pale skin. I wondered at how I could be so lucky as to be here. Our chatter faded.

I knew I ought to kiss her. If I was ever going to kiss a girl, a proper kiss, it was going to be now. If I didn't, I might never get the chance again. But did she like me? Did she want me to kiss her? I lay on my back beside the loveliest-looking girl in the entire world and found that I couldn't move. I was paralysed with indecision. A sickening panic grew in my stomach and soon I could hardly even speak. I have no idea how long we lay there. But then a cloud came over, and in the chill Sally sat up and hugged her knees. It was getting cold. Could we get on?

I said OK. And in the distance I heard that bloody sandpiper cry from the opposite shore and I shuddered.

We walked on in silence. I felt wretched and nauseous. I tried to blink away the sting of failure in my eyes. No matter what happened in the future, that one pivotal moment had passed. There had been a fork in the path and I had taken the wrong turning. That little fragment of the past would stay with me for ever. My feelings were all there but I was afraid to express them. Perhaps it was a fear of failure. Or was I simply afraid of my own feelings? Either way, fear had won.

We put our shoes on and continued along the shore. Out on the spit I watched the river birds running along the mud, dipping their beaks in search of food.

In the workshop I clear a bit of the bench and lay down my sketchbook. I stare down at the sketch of Connie's bike. There is only one

131

way to make a bicycle, no matter what size it is. Construct it bit by bit. Chas Roberts in miniature.

Bicycle making has a wonderful nomenclature, which I love. Each and every bit has its proper name. Let's start with the frame: 0.8mm wire for the main frame triangle, top tube (crossbar), seat tube and down tube, slightly thicker piece of tubing (or chenier in jewellery-speak) for the head tube (where the front forks fit) and also for the bottom bracket (where the pedals turn).

I cut each piece carefully with my piercing saw and file to the correct angles. This is a step-through bike so the top tube isn't exactly a crossbar; it runs lower and parallel with the down tube. I lay the pieces out on a charcoal block like thin grains of rice against the soft black. The angles are paramount. Even with fine tweezers, it's tricky. I peg the pieces in place with dressmakers' pins to stop them from moving about. Then a squeeze of syringe solder on each joint and a blast of heat, and it seems to be working.

The seat-stays and chain-stays are much more difficult. They run in pairs with a gap between, which has to be big enough to fit the rear wheel. And then to hold the wheel, I'll need rear drop-outs – the curving lugs at the apex of the triangle where the wheel's axle slots in. I choose much thinner wire for this, 0.6mm diameter. Days of optivisor-clad, eye-straining, back-aching, patience-trying work begin in earnest.

The wheels are so hard because on this scale the spokes ought to be microns thin. I experiment and discover it looks best fitting fewer spokes and making them out of 0.4mm wire. I build the front forks, stem and handlebars, which fit neatly into the head tube. Connie's steering runs on two sets of bearings called the head race and the crown race. I can remember removing and refitting these on my old bike in the seventies and have just done the same on a classic Holdsworth that I'm fixing up at home. No need for bearings on this little bike though.

Next I fit the pedals, seat post and saddle.

We need lights of course, so I cut a short piece of chenier about

2mm in both diameter and length and solder one on the head tube and one onto a seat stay. Using my micro-motor I burr out enough metal to hold a 1.5mm stone and drop a little diamond in the front setting and gently rub over the sides to hold it in place. That's my headlight. Then I set a little ruby in the back light.

I finish the wheels, texturing each tyre by rolling it along a rough old file. Prising the front forks and back stays apart, I ease the wheels into place. One of the pedals is near the bottom of its turn. It means I can stand the bike up, resting the pedal on a scrap of silver, rather as you would against the pavement outside a shop. I smile to myself. A bicycle is a beautiful thing.

Then I push the bike around on my bench, rather like a child with a new toy. All the moving parts work beautifully as I whoosh round a needle file and past the charcoal block. It practically steers itself . . .

Before bicycles, and before girls, it was go-carts. We took to building go-carts when our defence of The Old Parsonage became so successful that the Hall boys started staying away.

If they won't come to us, we'll take the fight to them. Armoured vehicles were what we needed, I decided. Go-carts, fully equipped, complete with harpoons, shotguns and hand-grenades.

The dustbin men were our best source of building supplies. They came on a Thursday and if we left them a note, they would do their best to leave whatever it was we wanted the following week. The main problem was that they needed paying. And they were grown-ups so ten Players No. 6 wouldn't always cut it. Cash was king. But that was easy enough to come by, in those quantities at least. We had newspaper rounds, a nice little business cleaning windows in the village, and we also sold the cigarettes we got with our forged money, laundering our counterfeits with great success. If we left a few coins with our note for the binmen we were pretty much guaranteed what we wanted. Eventually.

Construction of the go-carts generally took place in the old garages. First I hacksawed the wheel-sets from their frame. A hacksaw works just like a piercing saw, with the flat blade strung taut in its frame, but because the teeth face forward, it cuts on the push stroke. Slop a bit of oil on the blade, and the cutting goes easier. And you also have the pleasure of the most delicious smell of hot steel and burning oil as you cut.

Me, working on a go-cart, in the early days.

Pram axles were great but never strong enough for our purposes, so I'd strengthen them with a length of timber fixed on with the biggest fencing staples I could find. I'd start with a good rummage through the old paint bucket in the garage, where a great mixture of rusty reclaimed nails and leftovers from previous jobs all got chucked in together – every workshop in the world has its equivalent. Nails are one of the hardest things to rummage. Not like nice smooth buttons or Lego or even nuts and bolts. Rusty nails stick together in clumps and scratch and stab you. The interesting little ones drop out of sight just as you try to grab them.

But I was lucky because if I couldn't find what I was after there,

I had another source. My father kept his fixings old-school-style: neat rows of jam jars and wooden trays divided up into little compartments just waiting for a pilfering child to explore. Such interesting shapes and sizes, every nail designed for its own particular purpose. Most were in steel (some shining, some rusted), but there were others made of brass or copper. There were still plenty of horseshoe nails, square in section and forged long ago by hand (some in our very own forge). Floorboard nails were cut from a flat sheet, and the Victorian ones had hand-forged heads. I had my favourites. I loved the copper riveting nails with their domed roves – perfect little washers – just for their colour and the way your fingers tasted after sifting through them. And fencing staples, those strong, galvanised U-shaped steel nails, the length of a boy's little finger, designed to attach a wire to a post. I'd find the right size in the end. The nail store at The Old Parsonage was a joy for me and I miss it to this day.

My initial designs turned out to be based on a flawed concept. A heavily armoured go-cart proved both too slow and too cumbersome. As soon as we left the grounds of The Old Parsonage and entered Hall boy territory we became vulnerable. Up to this point our struggle had been territorial, our strength from stealth and camouflage. We were unseen warriors. Although I thoroughly enjoyed the process of designing and building the armoured go-carts, they had no practical use at all.

There were plenty of hills nearby, so the objective quickly shifted. We'd build for speed instead. A fast, lightweight vehicle would be much more fun. The seasons passed and our go-carts slowly evolved from crude heavy boxy vehicles to beautiful sleek speed machines. We raced the boys from the village, but our stiffest competition came from the children of teachers at Woolverstone Hall. The Hudson boys. They were not technically The Enemy. They were friends, and they were extremely smart. They made fearsomely fast machines and they knew how to ride them. To beat the Hudson boys, I had to build something really special.

The secret of go-cart construction is in the wheels. The back wheels take most weight so they're the critical ones. A big set of wheels from a posh Mary Poppins pram was as good as you could get. Smaller wheels from a more modern pram would do on the front, and they made it easy to steer, but if you could get really big on the back and medium big on the front, the thing went like a rocket. The only drawback was that the really big wheels were slightly weaker on sharp corners, liable to twist and collapse in extreme conditions. It took months and months of notes and payments for the binmen to leave exactly the right wheels. A beautiful old navy blue perambulator slung on a sprung steel frame with both sets of wheels intact. Each pair was fixed to an axle and welded to the frame. One set was much bigger than the other and on a longer axle. The spokes were taut and they had solid white tyres. Perfect.

The central plank had to be long and strong enough to support two (there was always a pusher and a steerer) but not so solid as to add unnecessary weight. The biggest wheels – ideally about 60cm across – were placed at the back on a supporting piece of wood. Between them, I'd usually make a little dickie seat for the pusher. The driver's seat was about two-thirds of the way back, built of plywood with sides and a back. If I could lay my hands on the right fabric, I'd even upholster the driver's seat. The front set of wheels were attached to a short length of wood, the steering plank, bolted at right angles to the big central plank. If you sat in the driver's seat you could put your feet on it and steer with your legs. This was good on rough ground, or for sharp and sudden manoeuvres. Otherwise the driver sat back and steered with his hands, using a loop of rope tied to either end of the steering plank.

I remember sawing with long, slow strokes, using the whole blade. This was to be my fastest go-cart yet so out of respect I sanded every surface by hand, smoothing off corners and releasing the wood's fresh piney scent. The next innovation was to add a few greased-up washers to the 4-inch coach-bolt I pushed through once I'd lined up the holes in the main plank and the steering plank. The idea was to make the steering more fluid.

There was no need for a dickie seat this time, so I moved the light-weight driving seat further back to make the steering lighter still. The seat had no sides or padding. This was a sports machine. Then I added a couple of foot rests, one with a pedal connected to a lever on the back wheel, to serve as a rough friction brake. Press down with your foot and a lever would be pulled against the rear wheel with enough force to stop you in an emergency (or at least to slow you down). I tied a loop of soft sash-window cord to either end of the front wheel axles. Hand-steering only. I sat down and tested it, making sure the length was just right. Lifted up the front and spun the wheels with satisfaction. Then I stood back to admire my work. It was certainly looking the part.

Eyes widen each morning when the post arrives. Waiting for the castings to come back can take three or four days, or well over a week. It all depends on how busy the casters are, and how tricky the moulds have proved to cut. Nobody ever says anything, but there's an air of tentative anticipation in the workshop. You never know if a new piece will work, or whether it may come back slightly different, changed in some mysterious, undefinable way. We stay quiet about this, but we're all thinking the same thing.

When they do arrive, I often sneak off to my bench and open the packets furtively, on my own, wanting to check the castings myself before anyone else gets a look. The different pieces each arrive in their own little resealable plastic bag. I quickly sift through them.

You can see immediately if the casting has been successful. No ugly undercuts, clear crisp lines and all the detail intact. They are white, a pearly silvery white, and they have the sprues still attached, the channels through which the molten silver flowed down into the mould during the casting. Each sprue has become a short piece of rod, round, about 3mm thick and 1cm long, which will need to be removed.

By now the secret is out and there's a huddle gathering around me. I move everything onto the central table where we can all get a better look, and six or seven of us start opening the bags to look each piece over carefully, to see what needs to be done. There are sounds of delight and pleasure all around. Secretly, I'm hugely relieved. In this crisp white state, everything looks great, better than the originals in many ways.

Can we help clean them up?

They always ask.

No, I say firmly.

I need to get to know the castings and the only way to do that is to sit at the bench and hurt your fingers doing the job yourself. First the sprues have to be clipped off, and the marks they've left filed, then it's time for emerying, or more likely the micro-motor version of this process, which we call rubber-wheeling. I check each casting under a loupe, looking for flashing – the tell-tale lines where perhaps the two halves of the mould haven't fitted together quite perfectly, and silver has leaked out. Some pieces will need retexturing in places. Others will need hand polishing.

Before we get to that stage, I chuck the cleaned-up castings into the pin polisher – a huge spinning magnet in a box – into which I also put a cupful or so of tiny steel pins, and some soap compound. The magnet spins the pins, and they do the first polishing for you. It takes hours. I hate waiting, and I'm always tempted to pull them out too early, eager for the next stage of design. The more complex pieces, which involve more than one casting, still have to be constructed, though. In this collection, that means the bikes, of course, and a couple of tiny picnic baskets.

Ten little bicycles. All good. In fact, they look better than I could have hoped, even better than the original. Things look different in groups. Seeing ten of a new design turns it into a production. Craft becomes manufacture and that's what I love. It's like looking at cars on a factory floor, all lined up to be sprayed, or polished, or tested. It's trade. It's industry.

★

Our races took two main routes. The marina road, which I'd later cycle down with Sally by my side, had a good straight half-mile of steep sloping concrete road and some interesting side roads to negotiate. At the bottom was a nasty sharp blind bend at the bottom, just where it wrapped around the Cat House. The building on the river was said to be named after the china cat its first owner used to put in the window to signal the all-clear to smugglers.

Then there was the long circular drive of Woolverstone Hall, which snaked down and round in a great circle, rejoining itself by the cinder track to the church. It was beautifully tarmacked and had three steep hills. The whole circuit could be raced in two-man teams, the pusher hopping off and pushing on the straights or up a hill, and leaping onto the dickie seat for the downhill runs. For a solo rider the ultimate challenge was to attempt the two steepest hills on the Hall circuit and survive the hairpin bend that connected them. The steepest hill of all started just where an old disused avenue of trees met the tarmac drive. At the bottom, there was a crossroads, and it was the right-hand turning that you wanted. Right on the corner was an old Nissen hut called the Animal House, where schoolboys kept their pets. You couldn't negotiate that bend without slowing right down, so we had to choose between cutting in front of the Animal House on smooth grass or ducking behind it where the ground was considerably rougher.

Word had got round about the first speed trials, so a few boys from the village were already hanging around by the Animal House when Roddy and I arrived, pulling the go-cart behind us. Standing at the brow and looking down, I felt nervous. I wasn't sure how effective my footbrake mechanism would prove. Could those great back wheels actually turn such a sharp corner without collapsing? Roddy claimed the driving seat. Part of me was hoping to try it out myself the first time, but my role was always chief mechanic and engineer. And if I was sitting in the go-cart, how could I judge how well it was working?

It was a long run-up, me pushing, Roddy steering. As we topped the brow of the hill, gravity quickly took over. My legs couldn't keep up so, with a final shove, I let it fly. Down the hill he flew, leaning backwards, steering ropes taut. What a sight! It was superbly fast. This cart bettered anything we'd built yet. But at that speed there was no hope of making the corner.

Suddenly, to my horror, Roddy decided to pull right and cut round behind the Animal House. At break-neck speed the go-cart left the smooth tarmac and swerved onto the grass. Steering hard to the right, he was pulling on the ropes like Jesse James on his horse. I could see sods of earth and grass spraying off the wheels. He hit the first hummock, bounced into the air and landed, still turning hard to the right, still accelerating. A great mass of debris was thrown up as he thumped down. Flying down the hill, still gaining speed, he was now nearly halfway to reaching the safety of the tarmac of the second hill.

At this point he hit another slight hump, beyond which the ground dropped away. The go-cart went flying into the air as if in slow motion. My heart stopped. Go-cart and rider thumped down on the front left wheel. The wheel collapsed immediately. Its nose dug in to the soft grass with such force that the go-cart flipped and sent Roddy spinning into the air, along with broken wheels and torn-up turf. The go-cart flipped again and bounced several times before ending up wheel-less on the tarmac road. Roddy landed chin first, in a patch of stinging nettles and brambles, as heavy and lifeless as a sack of potatoes. I thought I couldn't move, but then I heard my own scream break through.

Roddy!

I ran as fast as I could, faster than any of the other boys on my tail. The crumpled body in the undergrowth didn't stir. None of us had a clue what to do when we reached him. We just stood round in a circle, gawping, panting, waiting for something to happen. It might have been seconds or minutes before I heard a groan.

Roddy! Are you all right? I thought you were dead! I wiped back a tear. I didn't want to look soft in this crowd.

And then he moved. Slowly at first. Pulling his face out of the dirt, earth caked into his hair and nose and mouth. He spat. And then the hugest grin.

Did you see that? Argh . . . that was fucking brilliant . . . ow . . . I want to go again. Where's the bloody go-cart?

But he couldn't even walk for quite a while. As for the go-cart . . . it was time for another note for the binmen.

And now there are more decisions to be made. I lie out several sheets of A4 paper on the central worktable and group the different castings into little piles. Then I collect together all the chains and hooks and fastenings and any stones we might want to use.

I start with the obvious. There are always some pieces I've planned to the last detail, that already exist as drawings in my sketchbook, complete in every way. So I place a bike on the paper, and drape a chain behind it. No, that one's too thick. I change it for a thinner one. Then I lay a tiny ruby and a tiny diamond at either end, the rearlight and headlight. Those stones will need to be set.

After that it's time to put together all the elements for the daring little mouse that has crept into the picnic basket. As I lay out the components for a few more pieces, a stone here, an earhook there, I scribble notes on the paper: *big jump ring*. Or *should hang loosely*. When I can't find quite what I need, I simply draw it in: a chunkier chain, or a longer hook. Soon it becomes more collaborative. Like me, everyone in the workshop is art-school trained, and everyone has their own style, but we've been working together long enough for them all to know how I oper-ate and what I'm after.

How about a ruby on the top of that cupcake, like a little cherry?

Someone else suggests a double-strand charm bracelet – always fun to put together – and then another has an idea for a huge long necklace, with a cup and saucer hanging from it. An ant here. A sapphire there. A cluster of oak leaves. A rabbit races for a gate. We all start to play.

Each creation is laid out and photographed, and then it quickly begins to get out of hand. We've got far too many ideas between us, and I have to start rejecting some, go back to the beginning, remind everybody of the feel and mood and emotion behind the collection. I have to keep it all on track, so that we don't forget the story I'm trying to tell.

April is my production manager. She cooed over the new castings when they arrived but now she keeps looking over my shoulder and shaking her head.

How on earth are we going to make that? she mutters, while the arrangements we discuss become ever-more complicated. The mouse has proved particularly popular. We phone the casters in a panic. We need more. And after a day or two, I've got plans and photographs for perhaps twenty or thirty different pieces.

That means we can start to make the actual samples. When each one is finished we lay it carefully in a black sample tray. At the end of this process we sit down and have another long hard think about it all. It's nearly always a matter of hard-nosed editing, and that's where Emma comes in.

This one won't sell, she declares confidently. And, *nobody is going to wear this.* Or, *we already have six pairs of earrings so we'll have to get rid of these . . .*

Of course I fight my corner for some pieces. But Emma is very astute and I know it. It takes a good few hours of intense discussion and negotiation, and finally we're down to two trays, with a good balance of necklaces, earrings and bracelets. Not quite as many rings as usual, but these ones are particularly lovely, so I'm not worried. The next stage is pricing, and then cataloguing, and then Daisy Bell will be ready to show to the buyers.

This collection is all about the wind in your hair and young love and escape, and behind all that carefree joy, something more elusive. An opportunity seized or lost for ever, the kind of chance that can pass before you even know you've had it. We've included a tandem of course, because of the song, and there are the hampers, and those

142

inquisitive mice seem to have got in all over the place. But it's the Raleigh Jeep which means the most to me. I bring one home and give it to Connie. It looks good on her.

The bike obsession came hard on the heels of the go-carts. Once again, we traded with the dustbin men and built our own from the parts they delivered. The village boys were off buying brand-new racers and choppers. Meanwhile I acquired that step-through Raleigh. It arrived one Thursday rusty and broken, and anything but fashionable, not least for a boy. That didn't bother me. I removed every last part from the frame, stripped the paint with emery and a wire brush and repainted it pillar-box red using boat paint I found in my father's workshop. I wouldn't need mudguards or a chain guard. Or even a front brake. I'd only be using the brakes for doing skids. I oiled the chain and the wheel bearings. The crank was OK. Three Sturmey Archer gears were fine for the gentle hills of the Suffolk coast. I did need new handlebars, though. Cowhorns. And these I had to buy.

When the bike was finished it looked OK. And it was fast. I was fast. I had never been sporty but this was something even I could do well. I could beat most of the other kids in a race, I could skid longer and, budding Evel Knievel that I was, I could even jump over two or three lads lying side by side.

The best place for skidding practice was the cinder track leading from our back gate to the church. The track was long and flat and the black gravel perfect for locking up your back wheel on a turn and sliding your bike round in great arcs.

We had been working on Roddy's racer for a few weeks. It was an agonising wait each week as we put in our requests for more parts. Each Thursday morning we rushed to the bins to see what they had left. Bit by bit, we flipped the drop handlebars so you could sit more upright, stripped down the frame and fixed the gears. Finally it was finished and Roddy took it out onto the cinder path to test it out. On his own.

When he returned a few hours later he was bleeding and bruised and carrying his bike in his arms, in pieces. His pockets rattled with ball bearings and nuts and bolts. Unfortunately for him a particularly nasty gang of boys from the Hall had been lying in wait. Their leaders went by the names of Scarface and English. They jumped Roddy not far from the gate, thumping him off his bike as he tried to escape. Then they beat him up and, to add insult to injury, they dismantled his bike completely, right down to the wheel bearings. It was a humiliating reminder that the war was never really quite over.

After bikes we naturally progressed to mopeds and motorbikes. Just the names still bring a smile to my face: Yamaha (shortened to Yammy), FS1-E (pronounced Fizzy), Honda SS50, Fantic (if you had rich parents), Mobylette (surprisingly fast), and my particular favourite, the Puch Maxi – probably the girliest of them all, a step-through moped with a little shopping basket on the front. But it was all I could afford. Forging coins and cleaning windows was never going to pay for a serious moped.

I stripped the engine and ground down the cylinder head to give it more compression. I built an air-scoop to force air into the gasping carburettor and I drilled out the jets. I stripped it right down to lose any excess weight. And I tinkered. Every day I tinkered for hours. Friends would bring their old machines and we all would work on them together. At any given time you might find half a dozen fourteen-year-old boys in a cloud of exhaust fumes, revving engines outside the old barn.

As a result my little Puch Maxi went like a rocket. Not as fast as some, though. There were Fizzies around which famously topped 50 miles an hour. We raced around the back roads of Suffolk creating havoc. You had to be sixteen to drive a moped legally but that didn't stop us. Occasionally I would steal a bigger bike and hammer along the curves of the Strand, the long flat road that follows the river Orwell towards Ipswich. I would pull the throttle back gradually . . . 50, 60, 70 miles an hour . . . hedges flashed by in streaks. I was absolutely terrified but completely unable to stop. Faster and faster, as fast as I could go.

On the second day out of Land's End we are already exhausted. There are three of us cycling: friends of mine called John and Lloyd, and me. A scientist, an actor and a jeweller. Devon and Cornwall are all hills and we are quite unprepared for their severity. We have chosen to cycle the picturesque route and we are carrying all our own kit. Progress is painfully slow. At about half past three we find ourselves at the foot of Dartmoor, looking up with horror at an angry sky above vast looming hills. There is nothing to say. We climb painfully slowly in the lowest gear, accompanied only by the sound of our gasping breaths. When we reach the plateau there is no feeling of triumph. We flop on the short-grazed grass beside patches of heather and stunted fronds of bracken, our bikes propped against an ancient stone cross. We are less than halfway to our next stop, with at least six hours of cycling still to go, and we have nothing more to give. By now it's late afternoon. The clouds ahead darken.

The plateau is actually fairly flat and it isn't raining yet, so we set off on the twenty or so miles across the moor. An hour or so later the horizon drops off and we can see the great hills ahead sloping down towards Exeter. Wild ponies wander across our paths and we take a short break so I can sketch them. At some point after Moretonhampstead, our little single-track road begins to plunge downhill, snaking its way off the high plains. We're zooming at last. It is a much-needed spur. The road is rough with loose gravel and stones and it twists and turns awkwardly. A relaxed freewheel becomes slightly hairy. And then the slope increases again and so does my speed. From 25 to 30 miles an hour. Great granite boulders flash by me either side and I have trouble with the corners. 37 miles an hour. My back rack is heavily laden, so the rear end keeps skewing as the steel frame twists horribly under the tension. It makes steering increasingly difficult.

But still the road drops away from me and still I accelerate. From thirty-seven to forty-three. A long way off I can see a see a sharp blind bend to the left. I realise that if I hit any of the larger stones on the road my wheels will collapse. I wonder if I would die if I come off at this speed. And then there are the bloody ponies to worry about. I hope to God that one of them doesn't step out. But this is my bike and it is a Roberts and it is built for speed and there is absolutely no bloody way I am going to pull the brakes. Up creeps the speedo. Forty-six. Now I am terrified. The corner hits me sooner than I expect and I fly round it. No oncoming cars, thankfully, no ponies, and by a miracle I still haven't hit a stone. Leaning at a stupid angle I cling to the road with my back wheel juddering out from under me. A moment of terror when I think I'm not going to make it, then the bend eases off and I'm back in control. I freewheel gently on for another few miles and wait for the boys to catch up.

Don't you ever fucking do that again. Lloyd's fury arrives before he does. *I'm not scraping you up and taking you home to Denise in a fucking bag, you twat.*

He is right, of course. But when I look at my speedometer it shows a top speed of 48 miles an hour. Forty-eight! I grin a secret grin to myself. What a fantastic bike.

When I first moved into my Elephant and Castle workshop, I shared it with a wood-carver called Jason Cleverly. He had one half and I had the other. Jason sat and whittled driftwood while I filed metal. We made things and sold them to shops and galleries. And in the evenings, if we had enough money, we would stroll down to the Beehive and drink a few pints of Directors.

Jason's girlfriend Kathy (who later illustrated *The Gardener*) had just returned from a long trip to China and we were off to the pub to hear all about it. While Kathy was in Beijing she met an English girl of the same age. They got chatting and became friends. Kathy talked about home and about Jason and she must have mentioned me because her new friend's ears pricked up.

What a small world. What a coincidence. She also knew me. She was from Suffolk too and she knew me as a teenager. She told Kathy about long lazy summer days at The Old Parsonage. About Roddy's boat. They both knew Jaki Prior too. And then she told Kathy a story which had stayed fresh in her mind since the day it had happened. She remembered walking beside the river twenty years ago. She remembered an odd memorial stone and splashing in the water. She remembered flopping back in the grass and waiting for me to kiss her. Hoping that I would kiss her. But I didn't. Then it grew cold and that was that. We carried on with our walk and soon after, she left Suffolk and now she lives in Beijing. But she had wanted me to kiss her and she said she was sad that I hadn't.

> *Whether she loves me or loves me not*
> *Sometimes it's hard to tell . . .*

Not long after my riverside walk with Sally Beaumont, men in suits started arriving at The Old Parsonage. There were hushed meetings with my parents. Dodo, my grandmother, came to stay with us for ages, and it wasn't even Christmas. One day they sat us all down for a *chat*. We had never sat down for a *chat* before. The strangeness of it made us nervous.

There is no more money. The bank is taking the house away.

My parents looked uncharacteristically worried so I felt I should reassure them.

Don't worry. This could be an adventure!

My mother smiled but Dodo told me I was a horrible boy and it wasn't going to be an adventure, it was going to be horrible.

We planned to hold a huge sale in the gardens and flog everything we owned to help towards our debts. One summer's day, as if in a dream, I stood behind a trestle table in the walled gardens of The Old Parsonage, where I had recently drunk tea with Sally Beaumont, where we used to set up the 'Bang a Nail' stand at the fair, and eat bread and cheese. Laid out in front of me were old toys and crockery, instruments, pictures, and a weighty old black-and-white TV. I had

Peacock

Once upon a time there was a Peacock and a Crow. Actually, more than once. There are lots of different versions of the tale that inspired this collection. From Laos to ancient Greece, every story plays with the same themes: vanity and envy.

The one I have in mind goes something like this:

In a world where all the birds and animals were still white, two friends were playing together one day in a field of beautiful flowers. Crow turned to Peacock and said: 'Look at these gorgeous colours! Wouldn't it be lovely to be as bright as these flowers?'

'Oh yes,' sighed Peacock. 'These plain white feathers are so dull.'

Crow flapped his wings in excitement. 'I've had an idea. Let's paint each other.'

Peacock agreed at once. Off they went to find the paints. Crow was the first to take up the paintbrush. Taking enormous care and many hours, he painted his friend in the most exquisite colours he could find. Magnificent blues and greens shimmered on the bird's neck, while a design of wonderful rainbow spots graced his sweeping tail.

Peacock was simply delighted. He spread out his splendid tail feathers and began to strut about proudly.

'My turn now,' said Crow, who was looking forward to an equally glorious transformation.

But the Peacock looked at him in disgust. It wasn't enough for him to have all those eyes on his tail. He wanted every eye in the world on him. The last thing he needed now was competition.

Peacock picked up a pot of black ink and poured it all over Crow, who let out a loud squawk of horror. From that day on Crow's feathers were black as night. But Peacock didn't care. He was already on his way to show off his plumage to anyone who cared to look.

The show of beauty I'm trying to capture in the Peacock and Crow collection is on a grander scale than anything I've tried before. It's a deliberate move away from the intimate, personal stories I've been exploring recently. And part of the excitement for me is the contrast in the tale. Juxtaposed with that flash of pride, I want a sense of inky-black malevolence – dark, decadent envy – a touch of gothic in Crow to cut across Peacock's selfish opulence.

There will be other contrasts too. Although some of the individual pieces of jewellery will be the biggest I've ever made, the craftsmanship involved demands work of the finest and most detailed nature, using techniques of delicate piercing and smooth engraving.

I already have a long history with feathers. As a child I used to lie on my back in the parkland between The Old Parsonage and the church, stroking my lips with a pigeon's feather and gazing up at the huge Suffolk sky. I collected birds' wings too, a sybaritic pleasure. I loved the feel and the sight of them, that natural perfection of aesthetics and engineering. There were rich pickings to be had in the fields and woods and hedgerows all around: iridescent calling cards from passing starlings and slender curving pheasant plumes, tiger-striped. Asymmetric flight feathers – a mallard's, blue and grey; a goldfinch, half-yellow, half-black. I used to save feathers from wild birds I'd shot for fun and others from partridges or ducks we'd plucked to eat. King of the collection was my jay wing, a flash of electric blue against black, white on pink – a hint of what Crow might have become had Peacock cooperated. The gorgeous jay is just the most glamorous of the corvids.

Peacock and Crow is another stage in a long journey to bring together skin and feather, something that's always fascinated me. My quest is to pin down the flow and filigree lightness of feathers in raw, cold metal. I wonder how best to recreate that soft sensuousness. A bird's wing has something about it that reminds me of the gentle curves and movement of a woman's neck and shoulders. I think about the lower jaw, the sternocleidomastoid muscle, the clavicle, the suprasternal notch and the supraclavicular fossa, and how they come together and move under skin. This is what I want to evoke: the mesmerising conjunction of hard and strong and soft and smooth.

Later I realise this collection might reveal more than I'd anticipated.

Did I feel envy as we drove away from the old house for the last time? The new owners were Lord and Lady something-or-other and they'd already been round with builders and tape measures and a brace of well-brought-up children ready to pick out their new bedrooms. No, it wasn't envy. Just an overwhelming sadness, mixed with a little anger. Betrayal, perhaps. All at once the life we had always known had been exposed as a show. A fraud, even, perpetuated almost by accident. Nothing would be the same again, and we all knew it.

I'm not sure if I'd ever really realised until then quite how different we were from the other families who lived in big sprawling Suffolk houses. They had investments, portfolios and land. We had existed by the skin of our teeth (and borrowing from the bank, I assume). The change suddenly made sense of the peculiar existence I'd always taken for granted. No central heating; not much food, either. I spent half the time starving hungry. We had eggs if the hens laid but sometimes for supper the seven of us would share a cauliflower with a thin parsley sauce. We hardly ever ate meat. It explained why I was always dressed uncomfortably in my sisters' hand-me-downs. But why, when I longed for a comic like all my friends – the *Beano* or the *Dandy* – why did my mother subscribe me to *Paris Match* instead? Was that part of the masquerade?

Our new house was called Cherrytrees. The cottage used to be the post office in Freston, a small village only a mile or two from The Old Parsonage. If I saw it now it wouldn't strike me as a small house – and somehow we soon managed to make it bigger, extending and spreading over the years, with endless lean-tos in all directions propping up the old building at its centre. But when we moved in, it felt like being squeezed into a tiny box. I just wanted to escape.

By then I was seventeen. Even Suffolk didn't feel big enough for me any more. The first step to stretching my wings was a foundation course at Ipswich Art School. Here we had our very own cultural revolution. On Day One, our teachers, who dressed in frayed paint-stained jeans and sneakers without laces, told us that they had just one objective: to de-educate us. They were determined that we should un-learn everything we had been taught so far, about life and art alike. Then we could start again, looking at the world afresh, without prejudice. It was an approach that certainly suited me at the time.

We all sat on the floor blindfolded, with sheets of paper and pots of paint, while freaky American west-coast hippy music blasted out of the speakers. *Paint the music man . . . Just paint the beautiful music.* So we did. I felt as if I'd spent my educational life so far in a straitjacket. I splashed and splurged colour in a horrible mess all over the paper and all over myself, but it didn't matter a jot. I was liberated.

It was around then that I started getting interested in clothes, not simply in a practical sense but as a way to express ideas. Roddy and I used to wear mohair jumpers knitted by Nikki in florescent stripes, so massively too big for us that they hung off our shoulders. Roddy was more ambitious than me with his hair. Occasionally we both wore a bit of make-up, eyeliner we scrounged from our sisters or girlfriends.

We had always made our own clothes at The Old Parsonage. Clothkits were the simplest: bright easy patterns printed directly onto the fabric, with little scissor markings so you couldn't go wrong. Cut them out and stitch them up. Cheap and cheerful but

Me, sitting on the steps, chatting with Roddy after an eventful all-night party in Oxford.

cool too, in a 1970s sort of a way. But now I learned how to design clothes from scratch. My sister Nikki was the inspiration. She was studying fashion at Harrow and would occasionally return home bringing with her a waft of something exotic: a black line outlining her lipstick, perhaps, wild back-combed hair or a baggy T-shirt pulled in tight with a heavy belt over cut-off jeans. She talked of parties where Adam Ant or Duran Duran might turn up, and the out-of-reach suddenly seemed within my grasp.

Nikki taught me how to cut a pattern and about the fabric itself, how it has a grain, about the nap and the bias, and how to lay out a pattern so a garment hangs well. I began to experiment with cut, colour and materials.

First things first. I need to find some feathers. One of my daughters has a vase of peacock feathers in her room so I borrow them for a couple of hours and make a few sketches, take a few notes, play about with them. I photograph them against a white background so that I can reduce the images and mess around with them on the computer.

I need a crow feather too. There are plenty of crows in the local park. On early morning dog walks you see them huddled and plotting, scavenging on the grass of the football pitches; later in the day they take to the trees. I pop down to look for their leavings. Of course, the moment you start searching for something, you never find it. It takes a few trips to every park in south-east London to find a good selection of feathers, and still I end up with more pigeons' than crows', not to mention several distracting bagfuls of interesting leaves.

But when I examine each feather, something's not quite right. I have an image in my mind and I can't let it go. The crow feathers I've gathered are as lustrous as petrol, but they are too lustrous. The grander the feather, the more perfect its shape. I need to find one with a slightly dishevelled look to its filigree, a particular humdrum curve and a twist I remember from my huge childhood collection. It's the kind we'd throw away after plucking. Tufty and disorganised and a little more wild. Where the quill becomes the shaft, right at the base, soft downy barbs appear like fluff. The barbs that follow look scruffy; they're not stuck together. And though the parallel barbs which come next are fixed together more neatly, running out evenly from the shaft, every so often they become unattached from one another and curve off in anarchic arcs. Rather like the contortions of my chrysanthemum petals.

I'm not having much luck finding a scruffy commonplace feather. Not until I shake out the duvet and plump up the pillows one morning and a little downy feather hangs in the air right in front of me and I catch it. It isn't quite right, but nearly. So I cut open a little bit of seam in the pillow and pull out a handful of feathers. Sifting through them on the bedroom floor, I soon find the perfect shape. A slightly tatty little feather with downy barbs and an anticlastic curve, it bends off in two directions at once, fighting itself. I make a few sketches and then I scan the feather itself into my computer so I can play with proportions.

Late one night at Cherrytrees in Suffolk, up against a deadline, I was hard at work bringing a concept to life in my bedroom: a fantastically layered see-through dress that would make the wearer shimmer and rustle like a bird. Bright confetti swirled with static inside pockets I'd created by quilting together layers of clear polypropylene film with netting. The bodice was fitted and strapless, the skirt full and flowing. Imagine a whispering cascade of stitched cellophane, alive with trapped, dancing colour.

Jaki was my living mannequin. We were alone in the house, and the dress was nearly finished. Jaki stood on a low table as I tinkered away, my mouth full of pins. I just had to make a few final adjustments. I stood back. In the dark, with the light behind it, the dress looked stunning.

Then the phone rang. The caller was on a payphone: I heard a series of beeps and the clunk of a coin being pushed into the slot. Then came the sound of heavy breathing. In the background the recognisable hubbub of a busy Saturday-night pub.

Hello? I said. Silence. Near silence, at least. I waited, listening to the sinister breathing for a minute, wondering if I recognised it. *Hello? Anybody there?* I didn't really want to know. I put down the receiver.

That was weird. Some bloody weirdo. Come on, then, let's get on with this dress . . .

But the phone rang again. I looked at Jaki before I answered. I knew it was the same man right away. His breathing was again heavy and laboured, but his time he spoke very quietly, in an uneven whisper, hard to hear. It was obvious he was drunk.

Roddy? I know it's you. I'm going to kill you, you fucking bastard. I'm coming over there now and I'm going to kill you. Do you hear me? You're dead.

Hello? I don't understand . . . I'm not Roddy. Roddy isn't here. Who is this anyway?

I know it's you, Roddy. I'm coming over and I'm going to kill you, . . .

The voice was chilling and full of menace. He sounded like a psycho. A pissed psycho at that. So I put down the phone. Jaki saw the look on my face, and when the phone rang for the third time, she picked it up.

I'll be there in five minutes and then you're dead. Do you understand? Dead.

Fuck off, wanker! Jaki shouted, slamming the phone down. She

155

didn't look as confident as she'd sounded. By then she knew exactly who it was, and I did too.

Oh shit, Alex. I think he means it. I think he's going to come over. What are we going to do?

Suddenly the dress looked ridiculous. Shimmering plastic peacock colours.

OK. Leave this to me. I said. And we both got to work.

I could only find four air rifles in the house, all .22s, but we had plenty of steel dart bullets, much more dangerous than flat-headed lead ones. Tom had sawn the barrel off his gun so he could carry it around with him. He'd had a quarrel with some lads from Holbrook village. When one of them was in a play at the village hall, he smuggled it in and hid in the loft behind the stage. As the boy stepped on stage Tom shot him in the back with a lightweight pellet, home-made, of course. He'd fell to the floor shouting *I've been shot! I've been shot!* It took several minutes before the audience realised that it wasn't part of the play and the police were called. They never found the gun. It wouldn't be much use to us now, unless it got to close range. We bolted all the doors, drew all the curtains and turned out all the lights. We had more windows than guns, but upstairs we opened four of them and propped a loaded gun by each. In the pitch-black darkness we waited, sitting by the window overlooking the road. Every so often I'd hear a rustle behind me as Jaki moved in the cellophane dress. We didn't speak. Jaki's rustling seemed to get louder and my mouth dryer as the minutes went by.

Perhaps fifteen had passed before we heard an engine. I recognised it as a Mini, driving slowly down the lane towards the house. The driver killed the lights before he reached us. The car pulled up quietly, with a rasp of handbrake and then a flash as the door opened and someone stumbled out, thoughtfully closing the door behind him very quietly. I couldn't hear anything at first after that, except the humming in my head, but then I heard a new kind of rustling, from further off. Someone was pushing through the bushes to get into the garden. I saw a faint shadow on the lawn.

The man stood stock still for an age, for so long that I wondered if he was really still there.

Jaki and I concentrated hard to make ourselves breathe. In. Out. In. Out.

We saw some movement down on the grass below, and a little later heard the noise of something hard. He had walked over to a downstairs window at the side of the house and he was trying to open it. I could half make out a shadowy figure pulling something from his pocket to work on the window. No luck. He stood back. I imagined him looking up at us. When he began to cross the lawn, as if making for the back of the house, I picked up a gun.

Jaki, you're going to have to reload as quickly as you can. I had never whispered so quietly. She nodded.

The lawn wasn't big and there were open fields behind it. As he moved away from the side of the house I could just make out his silhouette. It didn't make me feel any better.

I'd guessed right. This was a friend of Roddy's – or he had been. There had been three of them for years, best friends: Roddy, Andy and Malcolm. Until Andy was killed in a motorbike crash and sweet, kind, intelligent Malcolm had snapped and gone off the rails. In the aftermath, he couldn't cope. He started drinking far too much and in his drunken rage he focused all his anger on the living, mostly blaming himself and Roddy. It was Malcolm downstairs, and he was here to make trouble.

Staring into darkness, I searched for shapes through my sights. Black crosshairs were useless against a black moonless night. The stock felt cold against my cheek. I didn't know where Roddy was, but I hoped it wasn't anywhere close.

At last I caught an outline. I had him. I traced the shape of his body in my sights then up to his head. Dead centre. And I pulled the trigger. There was a muffled cry and the silhouette fell to ground. Invisible against the black, of course. But Jaki handed me another gun and I shot into the darkness where he had fallen. A yelp. I shot again and again. As fast as Jaki loaded, I shot. It was mostly guesswork but sometimes I caught a glimpse of movement and reset my sights. Soon the figure was crawling back towards the bushes. But I didn't stop firing until we'd lost him in the undergrowth.

A car door clicked open and a dim light came on inside the car. Through the foliage I could just make out a figure trying to pull himself in through the passenger door. We leaped into action again with a final rapid fire straight into the light. The sound changed to metal on metal, before the door slammed shut and the smudge of light was extinguished. The car started up and it zoomed off, back in the direction it had come from. I reloaded again, and followed its path with more shots until it was well out of range.

Standing in the silent darkness of the house, chilled by the open windows, I turned to Jaki.

I've had enough of this dump. I'm moving to London.

In the studio, surrounded by sketches and scans, photographs and feathers, I start to design the shapes of the peacock and the crow feathers. I want to make a good range of sizes for each, varying from about 10mm to 50mm in length. I'll be able to experiment when I come to construct the actual pieces of jewellery. I have seen far too many clumsy representations of feathers not to realise how wrong it can go. I know the pitfalls of this kind of work. These feathers must have that gentle, contradictory twist, and the finest of hairline gaps between their barbs. They'll be light and soft, hard and heavy. A little lawless if they want to be, with a certain freedom. But they also have to convey the essence of my original Peacock and Crow story: the opulence, the decadence and the darkness.

The peacock feathers I have drawn are quite open. Their long wistful barbs are barely attached to each other, except when it comes to the solid eye right in the centre at the top. The crow feather is much more dense, with scruffy downy barbs and broken parallel barbs. I print out my drawings, stick them onto a very thin sheet of silver and start cutting.

Two or three back-aching days follow. Each filigree gap needs a hole drilled first. Then it's just me and my fretsaw. Every cut has to be smooth and neat, for there will be no getting into these tiny spaces later with a needle file, no cleaning up after the main event.

Finished peacock earrings.

Look at a feather, and you'll see thin lines inscribed between each barb, where hooklets and barbules join and intersect. To etch these in, I start by using an engraving tool called a graver, which has a length of sharp high-carbon steel driven into a button-mushroom-shaped handle. At least, that's my favourite shape. I like a heavy cherrywood, with a brass collar if possible, so that it feels substantial as you cup it in the ball of your hand, sharp cutting tip in your fingers. Then it's just a case of digging the point into the metal and pushing. And remembering not to let your other hand get in the way. It's easy to slip and stab yourself. The best thing about the button-mushroom handle is the flat slice it has out of it, which means it doesn't roll away and damage the tool tip when you lay it down on the bench and go off to find a plaster.

I am a very bad engraver. It may sound contrary, but when I see that the line I've cut looks terrible, I feel something like relief. So the graver isn't the best tool for the job this time. Its mark is too smooth. It doesn't have the right texture. I want something softer.

Back in the design studio I have a closer look at a feather under a loupe. I need to get the measure of these barbs, and exactly how they connect. It's clever. Perfectly engineered trelliswork. Fernlike, each barbule emerges perpendicular to the shaft, to be gripped by tiny catches where the hooklet runs up and across. That's why you get that zip effect when you run your finger along a feather's vane.

This sends me back to my micro-motor, the little hand-held high-speed drill. I select a cutter (or burr) called a bearing cutter, the shape of a tiny Chinese hat on a shaft. I carefully follow my engraving and the smooth line becomes rough and juddered. It's just right. Now I simply need the patience to cut each and every line between the barbs, soft arcs which follow the flow of the feathers, sometimes parallel, sometimes crossing paths.

Paris again, and a little after-show party at the bar. It was early days in the business of showing for me, a time when I still shared a stand with Sian, an old friend from university. Nothing was yet routine, we had lots of energy and we weren't about to miss out on free bubbly and the sparkle of glamour. Those fashiony booze-ups were peculiar dos, everyone there as frantic as the next. We were feverishly trying to relax and release the tensions of the show. We wanted to forget about the huge overdrafts we'd gambled with to be there. We didn't want to think about the possibility that it might all come crashing down at any moment. Fatigue and empty stomachs sent the alcohol straight to our heads.

That night, that didn't help at all though, not for me. I just felt lonely and depressed instead. I was probably simply too tired, but being surrounded by beautiful people having fun seemed to compound my bad temper. And then of course I felt even more disappointed, frustrated at my own inability to join in. I began to hate everyone around me for having so much fun, and myself for failing to.

Just as I was about to leave, I saw the face of the most exquisite-looking

160

girl I had ever seen in my entire life. She was chatting with a group of her friends, on the far side of the overexcited, heaving barroom, and they were quite obviously all models. Even in that crowd she stood out. A peacock of a girl. Young, tall and slim. Perfect skin, no make-up, and with that air of confidence peculiar to the incredibly rich or the incredibly beautiful. Her eyes were clear and grey, and she had light hair, a high forehead, a strong jaw and an aquiline nose. She was the kind of woman I'd only seen before in a Dolce & Gabbana advert.

She made me feel more out of my depth than ever. I was an imposter, a gatecrasher. This was not my world.

Fuck it. I'm leaving.

I drained my champagne, and the music muddled in my head. I looked down at my empty glass, then back to the girl. Across the room she was unpopping another bottle of champagne. I watched her as she tentatively eased the cork out with her thumbs, holding the bottle away and squinting in anticipation of the bang. Through the noise, I heard the cork pop. But instead of flinching, she calmly raised her eyes and fixed me with a look.

I was paralysed by it. And then a moment later . . . *plop!* The cork landed in my empty glass.

When I looked towards the girl again, she was still staring at me but now she was smiling. Every romantic cliché came into play at once. I felt transformed. Everything else evaporated. The noise and the people; my tiredness and depression. I walked straight across the room and said hello in my best French. (Thank God for *Paris Match*.)

Salut. Tu veux quelque chose à boire? she replied.

And I did. I badly wanted a glass of that newly opened champagne and I wanted her to pour it for me.

Her name was Johanna and we arranged to meet the following day.

I'm working on the little feather first, the one I pulled from my pillow, soldering now instead of engraving. I solder half-round tapered wire onto my cut-out, gently curving it to form quill and shaft. The wire is so thin that when the solder melts, it is sucked

161

down onto the feather by the capillary strength of the molten metal. Even after adding the quill, my feather looks too flat. I need to work on that anticlastic form, shape it in such a way that it curves on two planes – a curving curve, if you like. It's a pattern that's both natural and mathematical, suggestive of order and disorder at once. You see it in an unfurling leaf, a saddle, the spout of a beaten metal jug.

The quickest way to create that movement here will be to make a couple of formers and squeeze the feather between them. It's a prospect that cheers me immediately. I love making special tools for particular jobs and I have drawers full of them, some of which are still used all the time, others not for decades. There are hammers in daily use which I turned on a lathe at college, hand-forged repoussé punches, and most recently a very successful clamp I made to hold pearls while we filed their backs flat in order to be able to glue them.

I'll need a relatively soft material to bend a tiny silver feather. Not too soft, though. Boxwood, I decide, and then start to hunt through my wood store. I'm pretty certain I've got the right thing hoarded away somewhere. Yes – I pull out a handful of old boxwood punches like a fistful of Cuban cigars. Drawing the curve of the quill onto the first piece of wood, I file either side of the centre line away into a shallow V-section. On the second punch I file exactly the same shape in reverse, so the two fit perfectly into each other. I clamp one punch into the vice and carefully lay my feather on it. Then I hold the second punch on top and, mallet in hand, I give it a whack.

A pot of buff-sticks (pieces of wood covered with emery paper) in the Elephant and Castle workshop.

162

A rack of hammers in my workshop.

Placing the little feather on my bench in front of me, I take a long look at it. It's almost as if someone has just plumped up a great big silver pillow and one feather has escaped and floated down to settle where it lies on my workbench. Success. I carefully unclamp the boxwood punches and put them neatly in my bottom drawer, wondering if I'll ever use them again.

It didn't seem real when we met and it didn't seem any more real when Johanna and I walked through the Tuileries the next morning. Pleached trees, hoggin paths and fast-scudding white clouds across a spring-blue sky. I was the Dauphin out promenading with Marie-Antoinette. I was Henry of Navarre meeting my Marguerite. We strolled towards a group of old men, *boules* players discussing a point. Their chatter tailed off as we approached and they stood and gawped as Johanna floated by. I could swear there were twelve solid plops as they each dropped their boules in astonishment. I think I even heard a sigh. It reminded me of the song 'The Girl from Ipanema', and I was pretty sure that every person she passed went, 'ah'.

We strolled past beautifully planted beds of nicotiana, burgundy and cream against green. Men stared and women glared. Leaving the gardens, we crossed the Pont Royal and walked south along the Rue du Bac. The road is long and narrow but right at the far end, past the Metro station and past Rue de Babylone, there is rather a plain stone wall on your right. It has low, barred windows and a dark wooden-arched doorway. It's a secret place that you could easily miss: the Chapelle Notre Dame de la Médaille Miraculeuse. On this very spot in 1830, the Blessed Virgin appeared to a novice called Catherine Labouré, one of the Daughters of Charity. She gave her a medal, which came to be known as miraculous. Johanna took me there as if letting me into a secret.

We pushed open the heavy door and stepped through into a hushed courtyard. Then through a side door and into a kind of ante-room, which led into the chapel itself. Inside was lush, hushed and mysterious. Frescoed walls, gold, marble and Virgin Mary blues. Johanna crossed herself as we entered, then she knelt down at a pew to pray. This just added to her allure for me – I find the rituals of Catholicism fascinating. I looked round like a common tourist, and then we both lit candles. Johanna seemed to make a little prayer as she lit hers. I just pretended and tried to look thoughtful.

The gift shop was a shining cornucopia of trinkets, and the miraculous medals cheaply mass-produced ovals not much bigger than a fingernail. The Virgin Mary stands on a sphere, crushing a serpent's head. She holds her hands out by her sides, palms facing out, beams of holy light radiating from them. An inscription in French reads: *O Mary, conceived without sin, pray for us who have recourse to you.*

On the back is a capital M entwined with a cross, twelve stars – for the twelve Apostles – and two tiny flaming hearts. One is wrapped in a crown of thorns – the Sacred Heart, who died for our sins. The other is bleeding, pierced by a sword: the Immaculate Heart, who intercedes for us. The detail is superb.

164

The medals are described as *miraculeuse, lumineuse et douloureuse* – miraculous, radiant and sorrowful. Miraculous because they were thought to have protected so many from a terrible outbreak of cholera in the 1830s. Radiant because the immaculate Virgin Mary is depicted wearing bejewelled rings on her fingers from which a light shines, radiating from the gemstones down onto the earth. Sorrowfulness is shown in the hearts on the back.

I loved these little medals and bought several, unconvinced that they would offer me any kind of protection. But the shop was also full of other tokens. A whole host of little medals, some antiqued and some enamelled, mostly in that lovely Mary blue but some in yellows and oranges, translucent so the images below were revealed. I bought several rosaries as well, to hang beside my grandmother's above my workbench.

We left the chapel and stepped out into the sunlight, heading for the Luxembourg Gardens. By now I had grown used to the way people stared at us. After all, they were mere mortals. I, on the other hand, was walking with an angel. We found a quiet spot and sat down on the grass until a park keeper spotted us. *Pelouse interdite!* He chased us out of the park, while we laughed like drains. Then it rained. A sudden springtime shower sluicing out of the sunshine, making us dash for cover and huddle close together in a doorway on Rue de Vaugirard. We dried off in a café on Boulevard Saint-Germain where, over coffee, Johanna showed me her book.

There's nothing unusual about a model carrying her book – a small, black-bound mini-portfolio of 8- by 10-inch photos and pages torn from magazines to show off her best work. You never know when you might be called to a casting. I leafed through it, lustfully, aware of Johanna's eyes on me. She looked more and more gorgeous in each one, and seemed to wear fewer and fewer clothes. If this was courtship, I approved. Beauty was everything to me.

I turned another page. There she was in black and white, wearing nothing but a pair of knickers. She stood there looking defiantly into

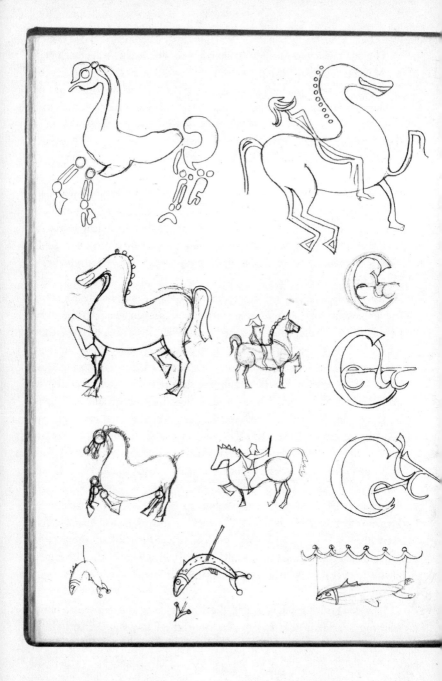

The Art of Dialling

EQUATORIAL DIAL
ALEX MONROE

To make a stick + shadow Sundial -
converted into an Horizontal Dial.

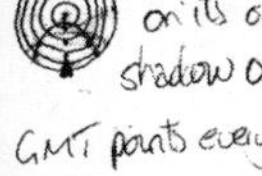

at a dist of wood, on adjustable legs, fit a removable stick (or gnomon). Supply a level + a stock of paper discs with concentric circles on. The wooden disc should have a moveable pointer on its outer edge. Track the pointers shadow on the paper disc, marking off GMT points every minute, when it nears noon.

The track will look something like this)

Pointer.

The Gnomon must always remain parallell with the polar axis. To calculate the angle ~~your latitude simply dedcuct your latitude~~ from the North pole (90°) the gnomon ~~is 145 the level of the ground~~ In ~~England~~ London (51½°) the gnomon must be at 51½°. On the equator. So if you are on the North Pole (90°) the Gnomon should be at 90° to the level of the ground. If you are in London (51½°) it should be at 51½° to Horizontal. and so on. If you are just using an hour line, on the flat, it has no plane so a sundial in

WRONG

the camera, arms by her side and feet planted firmly. There must have been a fan blowing because her hair was billowing wildly. I looked at the image. I knew she was watching me. My mind swam. I was drowning fast.

In my best French but with the strongest of English accents I said, *Wonderful lighting. Yup . . . mmm . . . great composition too . . . um . . . oh yes, I really like this one.*

Then she asked me if I had ever seen *Quatre mariages et un enterrement.* I was confused by the question. I told her I didn't know.

But the words must have meant something to me, for at this moment I produced a ring I had brought to give her. It was a chunky silver trinity ring, three thick bands intertwined into a sort of Turk's head. She loved it, she said. She rolled it onto her slender, tanned finger, where it shone brilliantly against her skin, the sunlight bouncing off it in blinding flashes.

Johanna asked me if I liked the theatre and I lied and told her I loved it. She had a couple of tickets to see Samuel Beckett's *Endgame* in an out-of-the-way arty place and did I want to come? I lied again and told her I loved Samuel Beckett. And I offered to pay. Secretly I thought nothing could be so awful it wasn't worth the pleasure of sitting next to her in the dark. *And after that?*

I packed up a few belongings and hitchhiked to London in the back of a battered old Ford transit van. A friend of a friend heard that the drummer of a band called Kissing the Pink had just moved out of a room in Leytonstone. I found the house, handed over some cash and sat in my new room, feeling very sorry for myself. It had been painted black and used for Satanic ceremonies, and inverted pentograms were drawn on every wall, so the first thing I did was to buy a pot of white paint and redecorate.

The next day I took the Tube into town and got off at Sloane Square. This was 1982 and the King's Road was close to heaven for an arty boy from Suffolk. Punks. Post-punks. New Romantics. You almost looked out of place if you weren't wearing make-up. I headed straight for BOY, a cool boutique where they sold clothes designed by Vivienne Westwood. I bought a massively oversized T-shirt printed with four words, LEAVE THE BOY ALONE, and a pair of black jodhpur-style trackpants with zips running all the way up the back of each leg.

London was electric. Prince Charles had just got married and Brixton had rioted (you could still feel the tension), while yuppies flaunted their new-found wealth. The IRA blew up a military band and their horses in Hyde Park and we had just finished a war with Argentina. Now Margaret Thatcher turned her sights on the unions. The police were the fist of the state and, as such, became the enemy. Out of this madness a New Romantic style was emerging, a softer evolution of punk, which suited me better. Not that punk was exactly dying out. Rainbow-coloured Mohicans made a few quid by getting photographed by tourists, and Rockabillies hung out at Camden Market. Hip-hop and rap had just arrived from America along with ridiculously large trainers. And I got a place at university to study jewellery.

I wasn't expecting to see a friend with Johanna when she turned up to meet me at the Metro station that evening. I disguised my disappointment and kissed them both on the cheek. Following them down the steps, I began fiddling around for some money for a ticket, but without a pause in their chatter, the two girls jumped the barriers and strolled on.

Um . . . Hello? Je n'ai pas un billet . . . attendez un moment . . .

But they were gone. So I leaped the barriers too and caught up.

We surfaced in a tatty district. The theatre was freezing cold, the seats were hard and I found the play hard work too. Four actors on an empty stage talking a lot. Hamm is blind and stuck in a wheelchair. Clov pushes him around every now and then. Nagg and Nell have no legs and live in a dustbin. That much I understood. But my French isn't really that good. It isn't a long play but that's not how it felt. When Johanna asked me halfway through if I understood

169

everything, I just lied some more and said yes. She must have known it wasn't true, for she then explained that the characters were realising the inevitability of their end. I sympathised with them.

Afterwards, in another café, the girls whispered to each other. Johanna's friend asked me if I was sure that I hadn't seen *Quatre mariages et un enterrement*. I said I was sure. Years later I realised they had typecast me as a bumbling public-school Englishman of the Hugh Grant variety. Johanna was as deluded about my attractions as I was about hers.

We met again once or twice before I went home. She popped in to *Première Classe* and we went for a coffee, arm in arm. Nothing more than that ever really happened, not so much as a proper kiss. It wasn't for want of longing on my part. But somehow the opportunity never quite arose. I wrote to her after returning to London. A few weeks later I pretended I had to come to Paris on business and we arranged to meet in the Café Bonaparte on the Place Saint-Germain-des-Prés. This time, I'd do things properly, I promised myself.

I was early, so I took a seat outside, looking out onto the Place with the church on my left. When Johanna arrived she was with another friend. This one was a handsome young man. He was dressed in the style of the internationally wealthy. A European version of the Ralph Loren Ivy League look, all perma-tan and Ray-bans. She introduced us and of course he was utterly charming, a viscount or something from Montenegro. I couldn't help hating him. They sat and held hands as I finished my coffee as quickly as I could and made my excuses, watching her sadly, my girl from Ipanema.

After we moved to Freston, my parents got proper jobs again. By the time the great storms swept across the country in 1987 the house was big enough to fit us all in with ease, and all but Tom had flown the nest. That October night a heavy bough from the massive elm that stood behind the house came down and landed right on top of it. The building works began again. The repairs were all finished by Christmas and the whole family got together to celebrate.

All four older children had returned to their new lives, Tom was studying in Ipswich and my parents had left for work when, early on the morning after Twelfth Night, the neighbours heard an explosion. It may have been an electrical fault or perhaps defective gas pipes. A fireball thundered through the house and within minutes the whole place was alight. The fire engines arrived to find the house blazing and thick black smoke billowing out into the surrounding countryside.

The firemen had gone by the time I arrived from London. Just a few policemen were there, filling in forms, offering my mother their condolences, picking over the warm remains for clues. About three-quarters of the house had been virtually destroyed. The top section had been curiously cut off about 5 feet from the ground, leaving a precise black jagged line between what remained and what had disappeared. It was like a cartoon. I stared at a pine dresser in the kitchen. Again, it might have been sliced precisely in half by a white-hot scythe, neat rows of cracked plates below, emptiness above. By the sink I noticed a puddle of white plastic, like melted candle wax, pooled over a spiralled electric element. A bare copper flex was attached to it, like a tail. This had once been a kettle.

One section of the house – about a quarter of the building – stood taller. My parents' bedroom remained, but it was open to the sky. Downstairs, I pushed at a brittle, charcoaled door, which still hung on its hinges. I saw a blackened soggy bed. A wardrobe full of clothes.

The fire made the front cover of the *Evening Star*: FIRE RAVAGES LUXURY HOME. One of the policemen told me that we could expect looters in the night. *If it's in the papers, they'll come from miles around.* Great.

Tom and I volunteered to stand guard. Sifting through the wreckage we found several bottles of wine still intact, and a good selection of spirits that had been lurking at the backs of cupboards: rum, brandy and Grand Marnier. An inky-black film coated the glass. We poked around in the shed for our old air rifles and gathered an axe or two. Covering the one remaining bed with a plastic sheet, Tom and I piled bottles and weapons around us. Night fell on our gothic nest and the pervading black grew blacker. Tom pulled some of my father's clothes from the wardrobe and we wrapped ourselves up to keep out the icy January chill. We worked our way steadily through the booze but the heady mixture of excitement, fear and cold seemed to ward off drunkenness. Lying on our backs with our nostrils and lungs full of the acrid smell of fire, we gazed soberly up at the stars and shivered.

The first car arrived at about midnight. We fired off a couple of shots and chucked an empty bottle or two but it was too dark to know if we hit anyone. They scarpered pretty smartish anyway. We laughed out loud and whooped. Just like the old days. It was the first car of many.

My parents were poorly insured. They stayed with friends for a few weeks until a caravan was delivered to the house. For a good year they camped out, doing as much as they could to rebuild the house themselves. I returned to London to get on with my studies, working every spare moment in bars and restaurants to pay my rent.

Halfway through my second year at university I spotted a girl across the platform at Aldgate East underground station. I had just got off the east-bound train and there she was, waiting for a west-bound one. She was carrying a scruffy A2 portfolio and wore straight-leg black jeans, black Converse and a donkey jacket. A dark blue sailor's cap was perched on the back of her head, not quite covering black hair with a bleached quiff, its streaks of yellow tufting up under the peak of her cap, except for the one strand that had fallen across her eyes. Her pale skin and dark black eyebrows and lashes had me completely transfixed. I couldn't take my eyes off her.

I stood glued to the spot on the opposite platform, staring at her unnoticed as she waited for her train. When it arrived I panicked and ran up and over to her platform, terrified of losing her, but by the time I had got to the other side she was gone.

I felt sick. The time was half past ten. If I stood on this platform at the exact same time every day I'd be sure to see her again, wouldn't I? So I did. Every day. It took a couple of weeks and finally she turned up. And she was an art student like me, doing her foundation course. Her name was Siobhan. It's tempting now to pass her off as Johanna's corvine forerunner – dark and lustrous, creative and mysterious. But Siobhan was neither a peacock nor a crow, just herself: a young woman full of doubts and insecurities and completely unaware of her heart-stopping beauty. I fell hopelessly in love.

Ipswich

Wherstead

Orwell

Woolverstone

Pin
Mill

Harkstead

Shotley

Stour

Manningtree   Mistley
              Quay

Wrabness

Harwich

Walto
Bac

Snape

Alde

Aldeburgh

Forest

Orford

Ore

Butley creek

Havergate
Island

Shingle
Street

Bawdsey

~~~

~~~

North Sea

towe

Holland ------▷

EAST COAST RIVERS

~~~

Lovebirds

A rummage in my scrapbox produces a rusty slab of steel. It's called mild steel, because it's low carbon and relatively malleable. Still, it takes an hour or so to saw it into the shape I need for a former, the scaffolding for the two domed halves of the locket I'm going to make. Eventually I have a chunky steel heart in the palm of my hand. I need a handle of some kind, so I braze a short length of square-section steel rod onto the back of it. That's always a hot job, but brazing, using brass, is stronger than simply soldering. Then I begin to grind the steel into shape with a sanding disc on my polisher, rounding off the sharp corners to make the heart smoothly three-dimensional. The heat intensifies further with the friction, and I feel the burn in my fingers. When I get to a point where I can finish off by hand with a file and emery paper, a whispering hush descends on the workshop.

All the time I've been sawing and soldering and sanding and filing, I've been thinking about the filigree. This locket is to be made of two domed filigree hearts. I've already drawn the pattern on a flat surface, but how do I transfer it onto one that's domed? How do I make my design work in 3D? Though it's easiest to pierce out when flat, the pattern will distort horribly when I lay the silverwork on the steel former to shape it into the birdcage locket.

I have an idea. I cut a piece of sheet silver much bigger than the actual heart and anneal it – a heat process which softens the metal – before sticking on a paper printout of the pattern, with double-sided tape. On the floor of my workshop stands a section of old tree trunk about the size of a large bongo drum. The square hole cut in its top surface usually holds a stake for forging silver, something like an anvil. It's a great dead weight to bash on or into and I cut it from the elm bough that smashed through my parents' house in the hurricane of 1987. Carving a rough heart-shaped indent into the top of this log, I now place my heart-shaped sheet of silver over it, pattern-side down, and hold the steel former on top. Then I whack it as hard as I can with a hammer. Whack! Again and again. I use the heaviest hammer in my arsenal. Whack! This is fun. A fantastically brutal way to achieve a delicate result.

It does take ages, though. As the metal is stronger than the wood, I keep having to recarve the indent in the log in order to force the

Me, forging a length of silver in my studio in Elephant and Castle, on the wych-elm log taken from Cherrytrees.

metal to bend itself around the former more accurately. If I anneal it again, the pattern will just burn off. An hour or so later, I find the printed paper pattern has miraculously survived, more than usably, and I snip off the spare metal that has concertina'd into a frill around the edge. By the time I've fixed the handle of the former into my vice and knocked the silver sheet back into place with a tiny boxwood mallet, it's looking like the heart of my dreams. This is going to be a generous, full-bodied locket. It's going to hang on a long chain, mid-chest, and it will layer beautifully with some of our shorter necklaces.

And now I'm ready to pierce out the filigree on my cutting pin. My confidence in the lovebird locket is growing.

Everybody at college was talking about the new exhibition. Words like 'seminal', 'revolutionary' and 'ground-breaking' were bandied about. I was as excited as anyone else as I walked off the newly regenerated streets of Covent Garden and into the British Crafts Centre in the summer of 1982. *Jewellery Redefined* was the promise. Here at last was the challenge we'd been waiting for: not just a radical response to the gold and gem-set pieces that cost a fortune in hushed Bond Street jewellers, but a riposte to their high-street alternative too – the kind of mass-produced fashion jewellery Gerald Ratner would soon be calling 'total crap'. The very notion of what could be described as precious would be questioned. New materials explored. Experimentation nurtured. Jewellery's interaction with the human form rediscovered. This was to be the 'Front Line' of jewellery making.

Brimming with expectation, I began to look around. The first thing I saw was described as a 'neckpiece'. Actually there were a great many 'neckpieces' here, of knotted latex, fabric and shells; wicker and weeds; cane and coloured cloth; knitted or woven nylon. A few bright lengths of plastic-coated sprung steel, curved into unfinished circles, announced themselves as 'flexible neckpieces', and a Finnish artist had suspended little printed cotton cushions from stitched ribbons and offered the piece as a 'headdress, necklace, waistband or breast-band'. I saw 'breast jewels' of copper and nylon woven into papyrus shapes, and a scattering of brooches, each one a plastic-headed drawing pin on a rubber pad. A collection of torn cinema tickets had been threaded onto a pair of earrings. There was a lot more plastic netting. One pair of artists had radically labelled a round 'mixed-media' brooch as a 'badge'.

I wandered on, hoping for the provocation I had yet to find. But it was all remarkably similar in feel. Things in plastic bags. A nod to voodoo with some twisted feathers, bone and leather constructions, frayed fabric on twigs. Torn paper. Cotton thread. Little of real beauty. So much for there being 'no limits' here at 'the first international exhibition of non-precious jewellery'.

My bubble of hope burst and I was left feeling distinctly deflated. It hadn't been that long since the Tate had bought *Equivalent VIII* by Carl Andre, better known as *A Pile of Old Bricks,* and its display had provoked outrage. The newspapers had a field day and people ranted in pubs for months. How could the Tate waste so much money on a load of bricks arranged in a rectangle? Who was to say what Art was? Naively, perhaps, I'd hoped for a similarly cataclysmic reaction to this jewellery exhibition. But as I stood there in the silent whitewalled gallery, my overwhelming reaction was one of boredom. The place was nearly empty. The few other visitors I could see kept their voices to a whisper, and studied the labels with great intensity. They looked a familiar type – a mixture of academics, teachers, makers and jewellery students, I guessed. This exhibition was preaching to the converted. The questions it was asking were never going to excite a wider crowd. They simply weren't interesting enough.

Coming in here had none of the thrill of descending into a nightclub full of New Romantics. It didn't make me grin like I did when I heard a drunkard raging against Modern Art. Or when I slid on those Vivienne Westwood trousers I'd bought when I first came to London. Here I was, studying jewellery at the art school with the best reputation in the country for the profession, at the start of a four-year degree course, and I felt more enthusiasm about discovering Issey Miyake's shop in Sloane Street and his bright red plastic bustiers than I did about anything here. I did try. I really tried. After all, this was my world. This was what I had chosen to do for a living. But there wasn't a single piece on show that made me tingle. I felt hugely let down, but I wasn't sure by what or by whom.

It was the same story at college. Although I thrived in the workshops, where I was learning all kinds of new technical skills, when it came to the way design was taught at Sir John Cass, I struggled. Innate contrariness combined with a hatred of snobbery made me kick against the elitist prejudices of my lecturers. Their ideals were outdated, I thought. Their approach felt prescriptive and academic, with intellectual analysis always coming before intuition and emotion. It made for a rarefied atmosphere – cerebral and exclusive, with little interest in aesthetics. As for the idea of fashion, there was only one word dirtier: 'commercial'.

I had moved to London for a reason. The creativity of popular movements was alive and all around, wherever you looked, and the buzz was inspiring. Young British artists had suddenly started selling their work for huge sums of money and they were proud of it. Every taxi driver had an opinion on the latest architecture. On my way to college each day, I watched the Lloyd's building taking shape, its peculiar inside-outness attracting crowds of onlookers. Out of college I devoured *Vogue*, where there was no shame in commerciality. But meanwhile, my own chosen discipline seemed to be languishing. It had stalled somewhere in the past and seemed unable to get going again. I suspected that I was being taught by the culprits.

Jewellery was rigidly segregated in the early 1980s, its distinctive groups set in their ways and quite uninterested in what was happening elsewhere. The glitzy Bond Street jewellers were all sparkles and diamonds, bound to tradition and stuffy values, self-consciously uninventive. Heritage jewellery. At the opposite end of the spectrum, cheap-as-chips reproduction Victorian engagement rings rotated mechanically on red velvet cushions in the musty windows of the high-street chains. So-called 'fashion jewellery' was sold on revolving racks by the checkouts of clothing shops. Cheap, plastic and imported, it was just a bit of disposable fun for accessorising a new frock. There were a few memorable exceptions in the fashion world, like the glitzy diamante costume jewellery of Butler & Wilson, just then gracing film stars on billboards, or Monty and Sarah Don's jewel gardens, which were actually paste in those days, and shrieked glamour.

The pieces on display at *Jewellery Redefined* failed to speak to either side of this divided world. Actually, I don't think they even wanted to. My art school clique only seemed interested in work shown in muted galleries full of unwearable objects with pages of unreadable text by their side. I wondered how Issey Miyake, Richard Rogers or Boy George would have got on in such a rigid and divided discipline.

Heading out into the real world, I felt despondent and confused. Annoyed, too. I wandered away from Seven Dials, off towards Leicester Square Tube station. Charing Cross Road was busy. I watched a group of punky young women waiting to cross. They were all dressed up and looking good: tousled hair tied up with rags and off-the-shoulder tops with bra straps showing. They wore St Christopher medals round their necks, layered with heavier chains and great big gold crosses. One had a mass of black-and-white beaded bracelets on her wrist, a rosary-style necklace and big black crucifix earrings in the style Madonna would soon popularise with the release of 'Holiday'. Others sported huge hoop earrings the size of curtain rings, or long dangly ones, and heavy plastic rings on their fingers. This is what jewellery is all about, I thought petulantly. This is where I want *my* designs to be on show. Out on the street, not in a stuffy gallery.

Street fashion in London is in fine exhibitionist form begins a feature called 'Peacocks on Parade' in a 1983 *Vogue*. A shaven-headed young woman in a studded leather jacket wears a big fake vintage pearl in a floral setting on one lobe, while a couple of crucifixes dangle from the other. Others wear loo-chain necklaces, home-made strings of beads, ethnic pieces mixed with DIY. These aren't models in studio shots. Like all the most interesting pages in the fashion magazines I've kept from those days, these vibrant images have been photographed on the streets of London, at the places I used to visit: the King's Road, the Wag Club, the Camden Palace – probably Charing Cross Road too.

Instead of going down into the Tube station, I kept going, thinking and people-watching. I walked on along to Regent Street and through the dark carved doorway into Liberty. Perhaps I was hoping to find some answers there. The whole shop was lively, vibrant and exciting. And the jewellery department was busy. Looking around at

A poor attempt at my first passport photograph, taken in 1986.

some of the designs on sale, I sympathised with the hopes of the exhibition I'd just left. I knew what it was trying to achieve. But if anything were to change, it would have to be from the ground up, here in the shops, on the streets, on TV or in the pages of a magazine. I realised clearly that I wanted to work at the coalface, for real people living real lives. Jewellery isn't an intellectual thing. It's expressive, emotional, even a sensual experience.

And why despise 'fashion' jewellery? *The groundwork for any redefinition of jewellery is not to be seen on a display gondola in Harrods*, critic Sarah Osborn wrote disdainfully in her introduction to the exhibition catalogue. *These brave first stages are too often beyond the eyes and experience of most jewellery wearers.* As far as I'm concerned, 'fashion' just means that it's made to be worn, not marvelled at behind glass, or kept in a safe. I'm not interested in jewellery or anything else that's created so that a small minority can feel superior about it. 'Fashion' jewellery is by definition popular, but that shouldn't devalue it in any way or make it ephemeral. It certainly doesn't have to mean dull or safe or predictable. Somewhere between Seven Dials and Oxford Circus, I became convinced that I wanted to share my ideas with everybody, not just a few connoisseurs. And I was willing to fight for that chance. With this realisation, everything suddenly became exciting again. If the jewellery world wasn't yet quite the way I wanted, then I would have to try and change it.

Things were going well with Siobhan, the girl from the underground. This was clearly not a passing infatuation. Far from fizzling out, the love I felt for her grew slowly and steadily, filling me up until I could actually feel it like a dull ache in my chest. We began to spend most of our time together. She had no parents and lived in a redbrick mansion block in West Hampstead with her soft-hearted Canadian grandmother, a Portobello antiques dealer.

There was always something new to discover in their flat. Everywhere you turned there were pieces of old furniture waiting to be restored, piles of enticing boxes, stacks of old magazines, a gilt frame without a mirror. It was dark and dusty and alluring, and you never knew if what you picked up would turn out to be precious or not. When the weather was fine we'd walk to Hampstead and picnic on the Heath, or shop in Camden Market for vintage Levi 501s with the right colour stitching. The rest of the time I was happy to explore, fishing through a trunk, examining a wrought-iron cross, opening drawers.

Then Siobhan's grandmother died. Siobhan was left devastated and completely alone, with the flat and a future to sort out. I felt needed and I loved her all the more for it. It took months and months to sift through every hoarded roomful. In trying to help, I often found myself forgetting her sorrow and mine as I rummaged guiltily through undiscovered cardboard boxes, like an excited child who has found a treasure trove. Siobhan was more childlike still. Stripped of her years by grief, she sobbed quietly as she sorted, every object she handled a reminder of her loss.

At last everything was gone. Echoing and empty, the flat could be sold. Siobhan got a place on a textiles degree course at Farnham. We celebrated at my bedsit in Clapham and made plans to meet up every weekend.

With new-found direction, I studied hard, graduated from college and looked around for a place to work. 401½ Workshops was a ramshackle tumble of buildings on the Wandsworth Road, where I shared a tiny brick shed with a potter called Pam Leung, and called it my studio. Acrid kiln-firing fumes mingled with the gassy scent of the torch on my forge, and clay dust got everywhere and blunted my tools. I just about managed to pay the rent each week. Another jeweller worked in the main building opposite – Carol Mather, from Leeds, who made little animated animals in etched brass – and soon her sculptor friend Jason Cleverly moved up from Devon to join her, carving wooden automata next door. This was Jason who later married Kathy, who went on to meet Sally Beaumont in China. Together with the other craftspeople in this labyrinthine building we formed a sort of family. We worked pretty much all day, every day, and long into the night too, sharing takeaways and tins of cheap beer. Occasionally someone asked us to take part in an exhibition, or a gallery shop would take a few pieces and hope to sell them, and we'd all rejoice.

Craft had become a noun, and although it wasn't quite Art, it was trying to be. The trouble was that everything I made was taken on a Sale or Return basis. If the gallery sold a piece they would, at some point, pay me. If not, it eventually made its way back to me. Sale or Return actually meant slowly starving in silence.

I couldn't go on like this. So I gave up on the galleries, and made up a small selection of earrings – hollow-domed discs as big as your ear, based loosely on Celtic axes and spearheads – packed them up and made my way to Hampstead. I emerged from the deep Tube station at the top of the hill, and wandered up and down the steep shopping streets, hoping to sell my wares. The owner of a little boutique called XYZ loved what I had made and bought the lot. I returned to my studio with a cheque in my hand and took the gang out for a drink. We sat in the Surprise with pints and crisps, and for me at least the way was set. I was a fashion jeweller. For the first time in ages, I felt I knew exactly what I was doing. But if my childhood had taught me anything, it was to expect the unexpected. You never knew when the next catapult shot might knock you flying.

★

It was gruellingly hard to make enough money to pay both the rent for my crappy little bedsit in Clapham and the studio too. I worried continually about my overdraft, which kept creeping up. I always needed a little more to pay for a show or to buy materials. I worked too hard for too long, burning the candle at both ends, existing on a diet of beer and roll-ups, with the occasional curry sauce and chips from the Chinese takeaway on a Friday night. I was exhausted and aching all the time. Eventually I dragged myself to the rheumatologist's consulting room at St Thomas' Hospital.

Ankylosing spondylitis and seronegative arthritis. Seronegative spondarthritides. You're HLA B27 positive. Is there a history in the family?

The words sounded fantastic. Almost fantastical. Even now I love the way they look when you write them down. But that didn't make it any easier to absorb what the consultant was telling me.

I remembered being told that as a young man my father had a bad back and needed hospital treatment. It was only then that I thought about his habit of taking himself off when things got a bit hectic, usually slipping away unnoticed to a quiet corner with a book and a glass of beer. I hadn't really paid much attention to the increasing number of whole days he spent in bed. But now his back was curved and his neck didn't turn.

Throughout my teens and into my twenties I often found myself gripped by the most terrible pains in my joints, and increasingly had to take to bed a lot of the time too. My health had deteriorated progressively and by this time I'd been living off painkillers for years, just so I could get myself moving again and back in the studio. From what I could understand, this rheumatologist was now telling me that I was fucked. There was nothing we could do about it. No cures, no hope, and no way of preventing my decline. No fixing it this time. Best just to accept it.

But I couldn't. I had never not been able to fix anything before. I'd spent my whole life fixing things. Making things and fixing things. That's what I did. So I left the hospital and limped home, where I doubled the dosage of painkillers and went straight back to work.

Not everything can be fixed as easily as a broken wheel on a go-cart.

Whenever I least needed it to happen, my body would attack itself from within. My joints swelled up and my eyes milked over. Sometimes I could get through by taking lots of painkillers; occasionally I was hospitalised. My overdraft steadily grew. A new treatment was talked about. The consultant wanted to bring me into hospital and try pulsing massive amounts of a steroid called methyl-prednisolone straight into my bloodstream. Rather like rebooting a computer, it was meant to knock out my immune system completely so we could start again. It wouldn't fix me but it might help suppress a particularly nasty episode. I wasn't keen, but after a succession of progressively bad flare-ups I gradually became bed-bound. Stuck in my grim bedsit in Clapham, I lay with misted eyes and a pain in my joints that was quite extraordinary. Through the fug of sightlessness, pain and medication, a ghastly depression took hold of me. For a couple of months I hadn't been able to work at all. The money had completely dried up. When the cartilage and tendons in my ribcage became inflamed, and breathing became increasingly difficult, I realised things were taking a turn for the worse. Eventually I gave in.

I was whisked away into hospital where I remained for months. Great hanging bags of steroids were plumbed periodically into my arms and injected into my eyes. I was a mass of tubes and needles. It all sent me slightly mad. When Roddy first came to visit me with a couple of clandestine cans of Special Brew, he was shocked at what he saw. A cannula in my arm had sprung a leak and blood had sprayed over me and up the walls. My vision was so milky I didn't recognise him, my body writhed and my mind jumped around incoherently. Roddy kept up his visits, though. Occasionally I would surface and see him sitting there, sipping a beer and reading the papers. He would look up and smile.

By the time I was discharged from the hospital I had no money, no home, and no girlfriend. In my absence my landlady had broken into my flat and cleared me out. And I suppose I shouldn't have expected

Siobhan to put up with it all either. I knew she loved me, but for her, the passion had seeped away. She spoke softly and cried as she explained. She was young and had a life to get on with, and I was stuck in a wheelchair. She had already been through so many ups and downs with me. It really was over. It felt impossible to contemplate. Of course she had done exactly the right thing, but it took years for me to understand this.

Roddy took me to an airport and I flew to Jersey, where my sister Nikki lived. It was the obvious solution, for my parents were still living in a caravan in the garden and Nikki's husband was a doctor who could monitor my progress. Nikki had always looked after me, and I'd never made it more difficult. I sat in that bloody wheelchair and stared morosely into space. I had loved Siobhan more than I had ever loved anyone before and now I was alone, with absolutely nothing to look forward to. An impenetrable all-engulfing inky-black cloud of depression billowed up around me and swallowed me up. My very life-blood had been knocked out by the steroids, cleansed of its history. All trace of who I was had gone, it seemed. I felt stripped bare.

In Jersey, I was just another child again in a bustling family. Good food, perpetual company, a sister's eternal patience and mild sea breezes worked wonders. Despite myself, I was up and walking again in a few weeks, although it was several more months before I could think of returning to London. My potter friend Pam kept in touch, and when I was finally ready, in the autumn of 1992, I moved into a small room in her house in Clapham. Pam had known better than I had what I needed. She realised that when I eventually surfaced from the pain and self-pity it would be my tools that would save me. Everything else I owned had been thrown in a skip by the landlady, but Pam guarded my workshop and my equipment. She smoothed things over with the owner of the workshops, kept the studio ticking over, and waited, patiently. My cold forge gathered dust and a thin bloom of rust powdered my pliers and hammers. But when I finally returned, everything I needed was there.

Making would mend me. Drawing, cutting, soldering, bending and polishing. Making.

I probably spent a good year growing stronger and learning to look after myself better, cutting down on smoking and drinking, swimming every day and beginning to make ends meet. I was still having the occasional attack of arthritis, and getting around could be difficult, but my parents had given me £200 to buy a clapped-out Citroën 2CV. With a disabled sticker I could park anywhere. My freedom was returning, and my horizons broadening.

Then Tom and I found *Swallow*, under a frayed tarpaulin tucked away right at the back of Webb's boatyard in Pin Mill.

We had been looking for a boat for months, something big enough to cross the Channel. We hoped eventually to work our way down through the canals of France into the Mediterranean and perhaps over to Cyprus. On holiday in Paphos once with Siobhan, in less dark days, I'd watched a stately old Dutch vessel sail into the harbour and the image had stuck.

Of course we didn't have any money to speak of. What we needed was a fixer-upper and *Swallow* fitted the bill all right. There she lay, propped up by cut-off telegraph poles on a couple of railway sleepers, in a sorry state indeed. We peeled back the tarp and clambered aboard to find a hull that had been partly stripped and bare wooden posts sticking up from her decks. She must have been abandoned halfway through an overhaul – a good few years ago, too.

Tom crawled through the fore cabin and popped up through the glazed fore hatch. The cabin would sleep four easily, he reported, and there was a fold-out table over the keel-box. Not much of a cockpit, but the counter-stern stretched out aft for about 8 feet with a great expanse of deck perfect for sunbathing on a sunny day, or sleeping space for a couple more crew-members at night. The more we explored, the more excited we became. *Swallow* had been built as a shrimping smack in Leigh-on-Sea, her cabin added some time later. With her stubby bowsprit, puff-breasted hull and long, slender counter-stern, she even looked a bit like a swallow. By the time the yard owner offered her to us for the price of her unpaid yard fees, we'd fallen for *Swallow*.

For the rest of that summer we spent every spare moment working on her, meeting at the boatyard whenever we could. We had a huge amount of work ahead of us if we were to get her ready to sail for the following season. Old wooden boats don't like to be out of the water for too long. Their timbers prefer to pickle in salt water, swelling up nice and tight. If a boat dries out, the wood shrinks, seams open and things start to rot. We stripped her down to bare wood and repainted. We riveted the hull and filled between planks. We fitted new beams and built strong chain-plates. We carved cleats from oak and constructed wooden blocks for the rigging. We learned on the job as the work went on, and saved whatever we could to spend on wood and paint and screws. No chance of an engine, but that was fine by us.

On Christmas Day, we lay on our backs in half-melted snow and slopped black tar and pitch on her bottom. Numb fingers and stinging, sticky streams of pitch dripping down our frozen arms. Christmas lunch was a couple of pints of Tolly and pickled eggs in a bag of crisps.

Throughout the following spring the boatyard slowly emptied out. *Swallow* was gradually getting ready to spread her wings too. Passers-by would stop and admire her as we polished her brightwork and varnished her spars. Expectation hung in the air.

Remembering what had worked so well at that little boutique in Hampstead, I decided to try my luck in other areas of London: the King's Road, Fitzrovia and Knightsbridge. I became a little cannier, keeping hold of the samples and taking orders, usually asking for cash on delivery. One stockist became two, then three or four, until suddenly I was busier than I'd ever been. Soon people started asking for new designs, so I made a whole new set of samples.

Stories began to creep into my work as I put together my very first collection: Fish and Bottles. (Not the most exciting name.) Inspired by those sketchbook drawings from the British Museum, and others I had made on a seaside holiday, I imagined a fisherman hanging his catch from a railing on a quay: forlorn-looking fish dangled in rows. My cartoony sketches had a slightly comical air, the starfish and seahorses looking absurdly depressed. But the shops loved them. Stylists began to ask for them for fashion shoots.

London Fashion Week used to be a huge and daunting affair held at the exhibition space at Olympia. Teaming up with an old friend from college called Sian Evans, we approached the British Fashion Council to see if we could take part. For the first few years we shared a tiny stand, exhibiting the jewellery on a home-made display built of canvas and plaster-of-Paris picture frames. From time to time, it would collapse onto our unfortunate buyers. At this point my slightly quirky, nature-based designs turned out to be far more popular in Japan and America than in Britain. As long as I had the orders, I certainly didn't mind. Within a few years I had an impressive list of overseas stockists, including Barneys in New York and several prestigious retailers in Tokyo.

And then one season Sian and I found ourselves dismantling the London show at breakneck speed, loading up my ancient Fiat Mirafiori and driving over to Paris to take part for the first time in what promised to be a very exciting new international show: *Première Classe*. My jewellery flew off to increasing numbers of far-flung boutiques, and before long I realised I needed a larger workshop space. A studio was available in one of the old Victorian workyards, the Pullen's Estate in Elephant and Castle, and Jason was happy to share it with me. Tom came to help us fit it out. Demand abroad and even at home was increasing all the time. I asked a couple of friends to come and help me keep up with the orders.

My work continued to be better known outside Britain until I encountered a very special buyer. For a fashion jeweller, a great buyer can make all the difference to success or failure, and I had a good feeling about Sara Dappiano as soon as we met. By fate or by irony, she worked at Liberty. Its jewellery department had changed utterly since I'd wandered in looking for answers in 1982, and when my own work first went on sale there, it was an instant hit. Sara kept beating the drum for me, and when we held our first major press event at the store, the fashion editors turned out in force. Their response was overwhelmingly enthusiastic.

I keep hammering away, trying to bend the British jewellery world to my shape, and probably don't change anything. But something certainly changes for me early in 2008 when the Victoria and Albert Museum asks me to make a special piece to commemorate the launch of their redesigned jewellery galleries. Another new door seems to be opening.

Born out of the enormous international success of the 1851 Great Exhibition, so enthusiastically promoted by Prince Albert and Queen Victoria, the V&A has always been a huge influence on me. From its earliest days, it has worked to bridge the very gaps I hate – between high art and low commerce, gallery and high street, exclusivity and fashion. It was conceived as an educational institution, with egalitarian principles at its heart – 'a schoolroom for all', according to its first director – where anyone could go to learn about art and manufacture. This was the way to boost both productivity and creativity in design and industry.

Now they are asking me to design anything I want, with no restrictions at all. Anything. Flattery and free rein: what could be more exciting? Even better is the thought that the old divisions against which I'd railed for quarter of a century might finally be dissolving, this commission the proof of it.

I visit the museum and wander around, neck craned at the marvellous high-Victorian architecture of the building itself, admiring leaf-patterned plaster mouldings, stained-glass windows, decorative wood panelling. As usual I make a few sketches and take a number of photos, glowing with pride in the fact that I'm not here as an art student or a visiting parent. This is official duty. I belong. I find no shortage of inspiration in the fabric of the building, and plenty of visual material to play with in its collections, but it takes longer to settle on a narrative. Once again, I am looking for a story to tell with this piece, and the one I keep coming back to is the simplest kind of all, a love story. The touching and elusive tale of the museum's namesakes, Victoria and Albert themselves.

So often it's serendipity that makes ideas crystallise. This time a phone call from Simon, my wife's brother-in-law, sets things off. Colonel Simon J. Banton was changing the guards at Buckingham Palace and wondered if we'd like to come and watch. On a bright Saturday morning in January, Denise, the kids and I hop on a train to Victoria, very excited, and I sing some very poor versions of A. A. Milne's poem. *Tumti tum, Buckingham Palace. Dum di dum di, something with Alice.*

We meet Simon in Wellington Barracks on Birdcage Walk and I immediately feel very scruffy. He escorts us in all his finery through the crowds. As we approach the palace's ornate black-and-gold iron gates, they are thrown open by several highly polished subordinates who salute at every turn. (I enthusiastically salute back and am asked not to.) We watch the proceedings from inside. Swords drawn and backs straight, the soldiers march up and down on a great expanse of brick-red gravel and shout at each other. White gloves, brass buttons and shiny boots, a marching band and plenty more saluting and standing to attention. It is a marvellous spectacle.

Simon takes us for lunch afterwards, through security gates at the back of St James's Palace and into a mysterious village within a city, with its own streets and houses, gardens and front doors. It's a whole world I knew nothing about: the officers' mess. I look up from the mahogany dining table, dripping with ornate silver and glittering with cut glass, and catch the eye of the first of the severe-looking military men of the past who surround us. As well turned out as our living companions, on all four walls these old soldiers stare out from gilt-framed portraits or perform glorious acts of gallantry in long-ago battles.

There is just one exception in this array of paintings. From above a pale marble mantelpiece at the end of the room, the sparkling eyes of a young woman in a dove-grey ballgown are also taking in the scene. Her soft brown hair is parted in the centre, plaits looping like spaniel ears on either side of a face that is pink, round and radiant, its slightly parted lips moist and fresh. It is a few moments before I pick up the clues to her identity: the royal-blue sash across her white lace, off-the-shoulder bodice, the glimpse of Windsor Castle behind the trees in the background, beneath a darkening evening sky.

The young Queen Victoria has just got engaged, to judge by the diamond ring glinting on her right hand. Her left hand raised to her chest, she clutches a blue pendant hanging around her neck on a cord. This is a very different image of the Queen from the one I know. Instead of saggy-jowled despair, I see a blossoming creature in love. She isn't exactly smiling, but she looks full of confidence, and happy – beautiful, even. Close to bursting with the joy of her still-unannounced engagement to Albert. No wonder those rosy cheeks. I am struck by the transformation of this lovely young girl into the figure she later became, horribly altered by loss and mourning.

The Mess Colour Sergeant, noticing my interest, is keen to tell me more. He shows me a small glass-fronted box on the mantelpiece below. It contains a circular blue-enamelled brooch, about 10cm across, three diamond-studded crests in the centre and a hoop at the top to take a cord – the very piece of jewellery she is wearing in the painting above. A little relic from a moment of happiness.

I am already fascinated by the symbolism and technical challenge of the locket form. The connection between a beautiful cage and Victoria's self-imposed seclusion after Albert's death is too tempting to ignore. Her story also brings to mind my favourite parrot, the lovebird. In French, the lovebird is called *l'inseparable*, a name I prefer because it describes their behaviour so movingly. The birds are not only monogamous, but they actually spend most of their lives side by side. When a bird dies, its partner becomes inconsolable. Often the mourner simply gives up the will to live, and dies soon afterwards. I'm particularly fond of the Fischer's lovebird. Male and female are indistinguishable: pillar-box-red beak and face bleeds into orange which cascades through yellow into a vivid green chest and tail, with a bright splash of blue just below its wing feathers. A rainbow of a bird.

So there I have my plan for the V&A commission: a single lovebird sitting on its perch, locked up inside a fantastically ornate filigree locket. It will be bigger than usual, its heart shape fatter and less pointed than a stereotypical locket, slightly closer to the shape of a human heart. I know there will be plenty of technical challenges in realising this design, but that makes it all the more fun to work on. And I quickly decide to hang the cost. To pay due homage to the Victorian obsession with the ornate means I can't afford to scrimp.

First there is the filigree, inspired by the sketches I've made in the museum's metalwork galleries: Gothic Revival choir screens and chancel gates made by Francis Skidmore for George Gilbert Scott. They are ideal for my purpose, which is to reveal as well as conceal. There is invitation in their mystery. Recreating that fretwork in miniature and constructing the specialist hinges and catches needed for the locket will be demanding, but not impossible. But I want to encrust the lovebird in a cascade of colour, tiny gemstones sparkling from red through to green. I know that setting such a rainbow of stones on the tiny creature is way beyond my ability. I will have to work with a highly skilled specialist setter. There will be a few small stones on the outside of the cage too, a glimmer of colour and sparkle to tempt anyone who sees it to look closer, to look within.

It was almost birthday season when the boatyard owner lifted *Swallow* into the hoist and towed her down the hard at low water to wait for the tide to come up and float her off. Nobody had ever remembered the actual date of my birth so family tradition was to celebrate it at the same time as Roddy's, towards the end of June. Later I realised that it was both unusual and inconvenient not to know your birth date, so I applied for a copy of my birth certificate, and in fact we hadn't been far off. But by then the tradition was set.

Late June produces the best kind of days, when the sun shines brightly but it's never too hot and nothing is tired yet. Tom and I spent that first night on board, dropping off to the soporific lullaby of water rippling against the clinker-built hull, and waking early to a clear blue midsummer morning, and the prospect of *Swallow*'s maiden voyage. Roddy was soon to be married, and about ten of us boys were setting out for a few days of maritime exploration, sailing out to Harwich and round up the Stour. We made an eye-catching little flotilla: *Swallow*, *Victoria* and a sleek sloop called *Rainbow*, skippered by our old friend and go-carter extraordinaire, Joff Hudson.

Swallow was the slowest but the biggest of the fleet, an Edwardian gaff-rigged cutter, with a bowsprit half the length of *Victoria*'s. Now she was newly painted in Dover grey, with a sliver of white to separate the topside from rust-red anti-foul below. Her bulwarks, the low rail around her decks, were rebuilt and painted white too. We painted little white caps on the end of her newly varnished spars. Cat's-paws, they're called. Roddy's boat *Victoria* really was Victorian. Painted white with a cream deck, her mainsail was cut from brick-red canvas, and looked splendid against a white staysail and a red jib. But *Rainbow* was the boat that drew all eyes. Another late-Victorian vessel, she was built as a gentleman's racing yacht, with a single mast and a single foresail. Pure white and fast as a dart, she was the epitome of elegance.

Everything was ready. I sent Tom for'ard to prepare to cast off and we hauled the headsails. I had it meticulously planned: haul in the jibs and pull her head round, then Tom could walk the mooring buoy aft, throwing it over the stern so we didn't snag on the rudder. Once we were off, we could hoist the main.

Don't let her off yet! I called out to Tom. *Wait till she swings round!*

But Tom was standing beside me.

Too late for that! We're already off!

Love Lockets

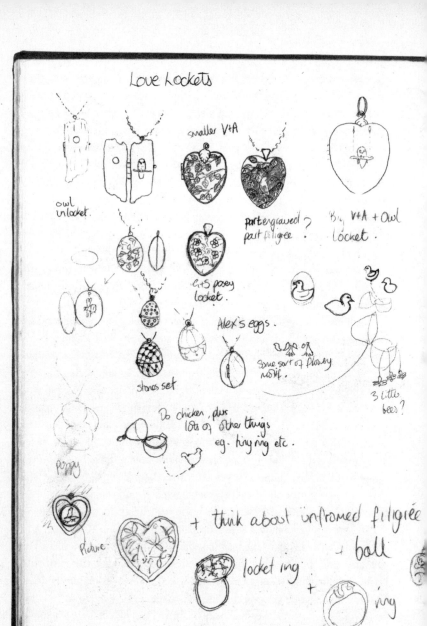

smaller V+A

owl in locket.

part engraved? part filigree?

Big V+A + Owl locket.

G+S posey locket.

Alex's eggs.

stones set

some sort of flowery motif.

Do chicken, plus lots of other things eg. tiny ring etc.

3 little bees?

poppy

Picture

+ think about unframed filigree

+ ball

locket ring.

+ ring

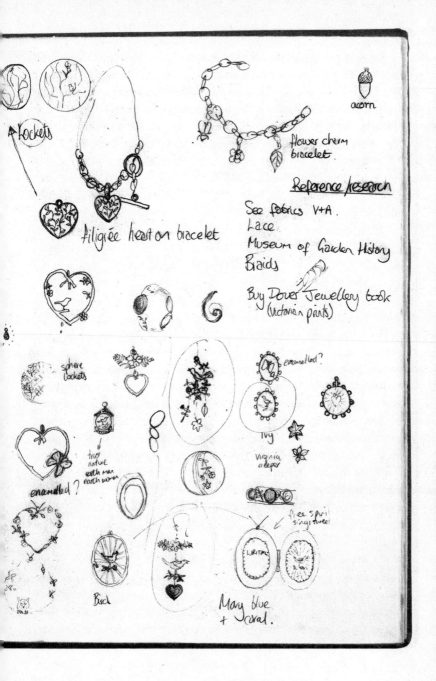

Lockets

acorn

Flower charm bracelet

Filigrée heart on bracelet

Reference research

See fabrics V+A.
Lace.
Museum of Garden History
Braids

Buy Dover Jewellery book
(Victorian prints)

sphere lockets

enamelled?

Ivy

Virginia creeper

true nature
each man
each woman

enamelled?

free spirit
sings sweet

WRITING

Bird

Many blue
+ coral.

I quickly pulled in both headsails as tight as they'd go to catch the breeze. We pitched to one side as she took up the wind, *Swallow*'s head came round gracefully and when I called for the mainsail to be hoisted, it filled like a soft cushion. We gently lurched forward against the tide, between the lines of moored boats and out into the channel. We were off, tugging our dinghy behind like a playful duckling. Shrouds creaked, ropes stretched and water broke babbling against her bow. Everything seemed to be holding. I leaned forward and tightened a running back stay, while Tom ran about the decks checking the rigging. We leaned with *Swallow* into the wind at a jaunty angle, rejoicing in the familiar clank of tin cups rolling off the cabin table and onto the floor. Tom stood proud on the aft-deck, brown-skinned, wearing only a pair of paint-splattered cut-off jeans, and we both whooped with joy.

Mine isn't the only new commission to commemorate the reopening of the V&A galleries. Grayson Perry is also making some pieces, but since he has no experience of jewellery-making, the museum asks me to help out. So from time to time Grayson pops over on his motorbike and I sort out any technical problems for him. He is making a series of little dolls, cast in silver and articulated like puppets. It is a simple enough job, cleaning up castings and fixing things together. I look forward to seeing him because he is such a regular bloke, incredibly intelligent but completely unpretentious: an Essex boy who'd hung out in the same London clubs as I had. I'm fascinated by the way he bridges the gap between Craft and Art, and Fashion too. And I am impressed by his down-to-earth approach and the accessibility of his work. I confide that I am nervous and not terribly looking forward to the private view at the V&A. He jokes that I should try wearing a dress if I want to get attention.

At the opening party I sip champagne and stand around awkwardly. The locket has worked beautifully and gone down well, and it is exciting to see it on display at the V&A at last, but still, I'm not feeling quite at home. I'm relieved to see Grayson when he appears, dressed – as I should have guessed – as his alter ego, Claire. But he doesn't seem to recognise me when I approach. It makes me feel a little foolish – like an overenthusiastic puppy, rebuffed. It's silly of me to react like that. Grayson is working and I've never seen him before in this persona – in a sense, Claire and Alex have never met. But still I'm disconcerted and duck out early, escaping off down into the underpass to South Kensington underground station and plonking myself down on the first east-bound train. I feel a bit of a failure. Why hadn't I mingled and chatted as I should have? The buzz of excitement on a busy tube train full of people on their way out for the evening makes me feel worse than ever. Then I glance across at the passengers sitting opposite me and I see something that steals my breath away.

A young woman is wearing one of my feather necklaces. The little feather, which I had once pulled out of my pillow, is suspended horizontally on a gold chain, just below her collarbone. It is the only piece of jewellery she is wearing. Attentive to his every word, she looks up at the handsome young man on her right and seems to laugh at a joke he's made. She has a glow about her, and he is beaming with pride, but they aren't touching. I guess they are on a second or third date. I imagine her getting ready for the evening, piling her blonde hair up on her head, doing her make-up with extra care, slipping on the simple silk oatmeal dress, and finally deciding on that tiny, delicate, golden necklace to bring it all to life. She looks perfect. And at that moment I realise that while the whole V&A thing has been great fun and exciting and flattering, actually this is what it my life is all about. I sit on the district line train to Upminster, and all the pride that I had expected to feel in the museum an hour or so earlier surfaces in me at this moment instead, at the sight of a stranger wearing my necklace.

With both wind and tide on our side, *Swallow* galloped along like a frisky pony. Past Pin Mill, along Butterman's Bay and Long Reach, we rounded Collimer Point, hugging the shore as closely as we dared, and then turned south down towards Shotley Point. Tom took the helm and Jason went below to brew some tea. The smell of gas and steam wafted up from the galley. Tom and I couldn't stop grinning at each other. After nearly a year of back-breaking work, our *Swallow* was a joy.

The river narrows slightly towards its mouth, the open landscape flattens and the wind sweeps across it. Everything becomes a little harsher. *Swallow* began slipping sideways, trying to turn into the wind and fighting us as we pulled against her on the tiller with both hands. A heavy-weather helm, we discovered. Out in the deep, wide water of Harwich harbour, she ploughed through the swell bravely, waves breaking over her bow. *Rainbow* and *Victoria* were already well out of sight.

Passing Shotley Point, we carried on out into the harbour before cutting just inside the Shotley Horse, a yellow buoy which marks the start of the deep-water channel into the Stour, the boundary river between Essex and Suffolk. The tide was falling fast now, so the going was slow as we worked our way upriver, keeping close to the northern shore. Once we had rounded Erwarton Ness, we could see Johnny All Alone Creek, sluicing through mudflats and saltmarsh into the estuary. This was a shoreline of tree trunks whitened by the elements and emerald-green samphire, curlew calls and oyster shells.

By the time we rounded Harkstead Point, *Victoria* and *Rainbow* were visible again in Holbrook Bay, neatly anchored, side by side, ready for the night. It takes a good hour to put a boat to bed properly. You have to prepare for any eventuality. We furled canvas and cheesed down *Swallow*'s ropes into perfect flat coils. We propped the boom on its crutches and mopped down the decks and just as the sun started to dip, we called over to the other boats and invited everybody for cocktails.

By sunset we were ready for a trip ashore. Three dinghies ferried crew and supplies to a thin strip of sandy shingle on the western shore of Holbrook Bay, where a few tents were pitched and Tom and I lit a huge driftwood bonfire. We wrapped potatoes, sweetcorn,

Our weekend sailing trip before Roddy got married. The flotilla consisted of *Victoria*, *Rainbow* and *Swallow*. We anchored at Harkstead on the river Stour.

chops and sausages in tinfoil and chucked them into the heart of the fire before setting off for the pub. Along the beach and up a narrow footpath to Shore Lane and then on up to the Baker's Arms, we took over the back room and drank beer until they chucked us out.

Back on the beach our fire had died down to a soft bed of glowing embers, cut precisely in half by the creeping tide. Little wavelets hissed against the semicircle of red-hot ashes. We fished around with sticks and pulled out some tinfoil parcels. The food was burned and smoky but utterly delicious. Then we talked into the small hours. The vast Suffolk sky always seems even bigger at night, and this was a balmy one. We lay on our backs under the Milky Way and guessed at the names of unknown constellations. The occasional satellite pottered by and every so often a cry of excitement went up when someone spotted a shooting star. It must have been about three o'clock when we decided to call it quits. Shore crews crawled into their tents. Boat crews rowed back to the boats.

Tom and I quickly regretted not hoisting a riding light. I sat in the stern, peering into the blackness, hoping to spot *Swallow* somewhere out there in the bay. As Tom rowed, I trailed my hand behind in the cool black water. About a hundred yards out, something in the water caught my attention. Tom paused his rowing and rested his oars. It was absolutely flat calm and almost silent as we glided through the inky black, both of us peering over the side. There it was again, not a reflection as I'd thought, but a shimmer in the bow-wave. I reached into the deep and as I did so the water around my hand glowed. I scooped up a handful. Sparkles of light danced on the surface as it dripped and splashed.

We had rowed into a patch of phosphorescence, and it was getting more concentrated. As we drifted on we swirled our arms in the dark water and the tiny bioluminescent organisms lit up like aquatic spark-lers, greenish-white light bursting out from our fingertips. We shouted to the shore and threw up great sprays of flashing light. Then Tom and I pulled off our T-shirts and dived overboard. I was dazzled as I hit the water and burst to the surface with an incandescent cry to Tom. We swam and splashed and shouted in liquid fireworks, brighter and more blazing than sunlight. After a while we just floated on our backs looking up at the stars, completely in awe of the beauty of the moment, the occasional ripple of light lapping around us. It was almost unbearable.

I woke at dawn to find the floorboards floating. I got up and worked the pump for a while, emptying out the bilges. There was still no sign of life from Tom or anyone else by the time I'd finished, so I stripped off and swam a wide lazy lap of *Swallow*, stopping occa-sionally to look at her lovingly, taking in the sheen of her paintwork, the glow of her varnish, the warmth of her neatly furled sails. We'd had a full year of sawing and sanding, scraping and screwing, painting and varnishing, and she'd proved worth every minute of work. She was a beauty. I climbed back on board by the bowsprit, sun on my salted shoulders, and stretched out on the aft-deck to dry. A wader cried from the opposite shore, its call carrying 2 miles across water that was still millpond-calm. No use trying to sail against the tide on a day like this, I thought to myself. May as well hang about here until it turns, and we can drift back downstream on the ebb.

What a day it would be. And then I remembered I had something else to look forward to, another kind of future. A few days earlier, I'd spotted a girl at a party in a vodka bar on Blackfriars Bridge Road. A red-haired pale-skinned freckly model. And I began to hatch a plan. Lying there under a cloudless sky, warmth slowly seeping into my skin, I thought at last that everything might be coming out all right after all.

An hour or so later, the smell of frying bacon drifted across from *Victoria*, and voices with it.

Butterfly

My heart slightly sank when Sara Dappiano left Liberty. Soon afterwards she phoned me, though. Would I like to make a small collection for the shop she was working at now, Coco de Mer? I was immediately intrigued, and we arranged to meet.

Coco de Mer takes its name from a rare double coconut that grows in the Seychelles, which looks so much like a woman's bottom that it's also known as a *coco fesse*, or sometimes a love nut. Even the palm tree's catkins are suggestive. On Monmouth Street, the shop is demurely but appropriately positioned next door to London's oldest French restaurant, Mon Plaisir, whose pewter bar first saw life in a Lyonnaise brothel.

Coco de Mer is a sex shop, and an extremely upmarket one, with glossy burgundy paintwork on the shop front, diaphanous purple silk and satin inside. When you've got yourself through the door, you're surrounded by busts dressed in exotic lingerie and racks of dainty undergarments with delicate straps and unexpected spaces. Jewellery displays sparkle against pink walls. There are also glass cabinets full of shiny chrome things, which I don't examine too closely.

And there's Sara with her long dark hair and olive skin, a provocative twinkle in her eyes and dimples showing with her smile. She's womanly, in a full-figured, sensual, Italian sort of way that goes with her low-cut flowing dresses. I understand exactly why she had moved.

They're after a range of sensuous, erotic jewellery for the shop. I love the idea. It fits perfectly into my philosophy of anti-snobbery in design, but also my belief that sex is something to be celebrated and enjoyed. I had wasted far too many years in my youth being overly timid, both sexually and emotionally. Now I find myself quite taken by this invitation to explore eroticism through my work.

The girl who had caught my eye just before *Swallow*'s maiden voyage was Denise, but at first the extent to which she would change me was far from obvious. I discovered she was a friend of Roddy's new wife Jo, and this meant that a meeting could be arranged: a dinner at Roddy's council flat in Waterloo.

Denise realised immediately that it was a set-up. She spent the meal with her back to me. It was all rather awkward, with the four of us squeezed around the table in their tiny sitting room. Every time I tried to talk to her, she became more hostile. I retreated into the kitchen to help Roddy with the food, and he raised his eyebrows and blew out through puffed cheeks like a car mechanic looking at a hopeless case.

Don't fancy your chances there, mate. He shook his head as he scraped the plates.

But when Denise slipped out onto the balcony for a smoke, I quickly joined her. Even under the broken fluorescent half-light of that council block veranda, she managed to look breath-catching. Her scruffy black leather biker's jacket was slung across her shoulder, over a baggy jumper, jeans and Converse. She was rather boyish altogether, tall and thin with short-cropped auburn hair, big eyes and a wide mouth. Her skin was as white as snow and covered with freckles and she wore no make-up at all. I thought she was just about the most beautiful thing I had ever seen. The flare in her eye, fierce and feral, reminded me of a wild animal. It excited me.

Seduction had never been my strong point. I lit two cigarettes, and as I handed one to Denise, she flashed me a furious look and muttered *Oh, for fuck's sake.* It wasn't exactly *Now, Voyager*, and Denise was certainly no Charlotte Vale, but at least she took the cigarette. We turned to lean on the concrete wall of the balcony. We watched some drunks arguing and the homeless men shuffling about in the dark street below, and I thought I definitely wasn't going to make do with the stars this time. I was after the moon too.

Despite Denise's fury with Roddy and Jo for landing her in it, I persisted. I'd had enough of backing off, and friendship was something I knew I could do. I wore her down in the end. I left messages, persisted, convinced her I was serious. There were more dates. Galleries and pubs. I cooked for her, fish kebabs on the barbecue. On my thirtieth birthday, a few months after our first meeting, she came to a party in a pub in Kennington and met all my friends. Miraculously, she didn't seem to mind when I introduced her as my girlfriend.

Later that summer I finally took her to Pin Mill. Barefooted and muddy, we dragged the dinghy down the Grindle, rowlocks clanking, and rowed out to *Swallow*. The boat now lay on a half-tide mooring up towards Woolverstone, 50 yards out from her winter mud-berth, which we had cut into the loamy bank the previous season.

Denise stayed in the sun on *Swallow*'s baking deck while I pottered about below. I lit the little gas ring, made us tea and broke off a couple of strips of fruit-and-nut chocolate. We sat on deck and drank from chipped enamel mugs. Then I had to go back down below to check the bilges. A year after our maiden voyage, *Swallow* still leaked badly. I pumped away, taking in the noise of the river, enjoying the occasional buzz of an engine or the full flap of passing sails out in the channel.

Surfacing from the darkness, I stuck my head up through the hatch to see Denise stretched out naked on the foredeck. She lay on her back with her eyes closed and her arms straight back above her head, basking. I paused, taking in the scene in silence for a few seconds. Red and white sails in the distance, *Swallow*'s golden mast and neatly furled sails, Denise's pale white skin and coppery hair, which glowed in the sun like the varnished larchwood of the bulwark. She swung an arm over her eye to squint at me.

I'm hot. How about a swim?

Denise stood up, stepped tip-toe up onto the bulwarks, one hand on the shrouds. Without a backward glace, she dived overboard. Barely a splash. I stared around me, partly in disbelief but also to check the world's reaction. Nothing else had changed. Sailing boats still tacked upstream, a couple of dinghies with outboards droned against the tide, and far off at the point a steamer was coming in from Long Reach.

A moment later I was treading water beside Denise. We swam right around *Swallow* and then up against the tide to see *Rainbow*. Then we floated back down with the current to the boat. We splashed and mucked around until we were cold and when we'd climbed back on board and were stretched out in the sun again, I looked up into the rigging and thought that one day I would marry Denise.

In the basement at Coco de Mer I imagine scented lockets and luscious orchids. Sara asks if I could also make some nipple clamps. I know my way around lockets and pendants, but I've never even heard of a nipple clamp before. I don't know what it might look like or how it works or even quite what it's for. So I nod cheerfully, go away to do a bit of research online, and discover that I have agreed to make a sex toy, which can be attached to the erect nipples of either men or women to restrict the blood flow.

Ouch.

I get to work on a selection of designs, starting with what I know. There's a Coco de Mer pendant – a miniature pelvis-shaped nut set with a ruby – and a number of lockets, including a large filigree butterfly with an orchid inside. Spilling from the orchid is a length of red silk, to absorb a scent. The lockets are on longer chains than usual, so that they nestle in the wearer's cleavage. The nipple clamps are butterflies too, rather like hair-clips, with wings that you squeeze together to open the claws. I sketch out a filigree pattern for the butterfly's wings, leaving spaces in the shape of a penis. Everyone at Coco de Mer loves the designs. Aesthetics sorted, I'm ready to make the prototypes, and now my challenges are practical and mechanical.

I've done some technical drawings and worked out how the hinge should pivot, but the spring is a little more complex. There are myriad springs available: tension springs, compression springs, torsion springs. And then there are different types of wire and thicknesses of wire to consider, and the effects of the degree of deflection, the number of turns, the dimensions of the mandrel, the position of the ends . . . the variables are infinite. I remember my Wednesday afternoons at university, studying metallurgy with the eccentric and brilliantly named Dr Choc. We experimented with hardening and tempering steel, making it soft then springy again, heating it and cooling it, studying its molecular structure. It was fascinating but, as I reflect, not actually that much use to me just now.

I decide that what I really need is a whole bunch of samples to play with. I find a helpful company in Redditch, and as I'm ordering a good selection of small torsion springs – think of an old-fashioned mousetrap, or a clothes peg, perhaps – the man at the other end of the phone asks me what they're for. I'm briefly thrown. Then I decide to lie and tell him I'm designing a range of hair-clips.

Back at Coco de Mer, I'm greeted by two charming sales assistants. A young woman called Alison tells me that her mother is a big fan of mine, and adores the lovebird locket she bought from the V&A. I'm flattered, and immediately put at ease. While I wait for Sara, I scan the bawdy Edwardian cartoons, framed on the walls alongside a number of retro-looking erotic publications, and keep half an ear on the crooning of Tex Ritter, the singing cowboy, playing in the background. The music seems a little out of place, and I wonder what that new moon over his shoulder is all about. Then a damson-painted door opens and Sara greets me with a kiss. We descend into the basement.

I feel the heat rising to my face as I squirm in my chair. We've been joined by three other young women, and the five of us are soon sitting around an overflowing table, surrounded by piles of paperwork, computers and sex toys. I nervously produce the working prototypes of each of my designs, and add them to the chaos. The butterfly, now plated in shimmering gold, looks altogether pretty and innocent. The spring is coiled round its swelling thorax, its six legs are exaggeratedly long and softened with small balls on their ends. Antennae swirl out from the head. The uninitiated would be pushed to guess the object's function. The penis design in the filigree wings is both blatant and disguised. Everyone leans forward.

Sara and her colleagues each reach for a clamp and immediately clip it onto their knuckle. They've done this before. They hold out their hands, backs to the ceiling, like visitors to a butterfly garden. The insects have settled. How long will they stay? I watch the women's faces. Something is wrong. They are playing with the wings, squeezing them together and repositioning the clamps on their knuckles, frowning. When I'd finished my first prototype and clipped the butterfly on the end of my finger, it had hurt. Worried that I'd made it too firm, I made some more using different springs, softer ones.

Which one is the strongest? asks Sara.

I gently clip the one with the most powerful spring onto the back of Sara's soft, tanned hand. Her nails are perfectly painted. Everyone leans forward to play with it. It's lovely, they agree. The butterfly and the design are perfect. But they also all agree that the spring is not nearly hard enough. My eyes start to water as I cross my arms casually over my nipples and say that's fine. I can use a harder spring. No problem.

It was Christmas 1995. Denise's mum sat me down on a stool in our front room in Peckham for some spiritual healing. Joan, she was called, but I never actually said it out loud, face to face. It's amazing how easy it is to avoid using someone's name. Joan was a medium. It was time for some diplomacy on my part as far as all this was concerned. After half a lifetime of pain in my joints, I was quite happy to play along. What harm could it possibly do?

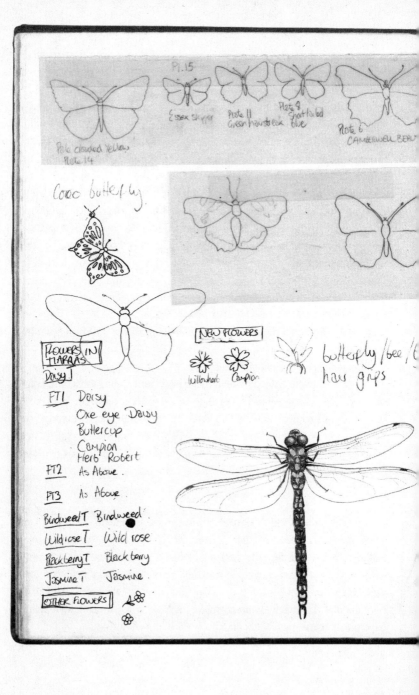

Pl.15

Essex skipper

Plate 11
Green hairstreak

Plate 8
Short tailed
blue

Plate 6
CAMBERWELL BEAUTY

Pale clouded Yellow
Plate 14

Cabbo butterfly

FLOWERS IN
TIARAAS

Daisy

FT1   Daisy
       Oxe eye Daisy
       Buttercup
       Campion
       Herb Robert
FT2   As Above.

FT3   As Above.

Bindweed T   Bindweed ●
Wild rose T   Wild rose
Blackberry T Black berry
Jasmine T   Jasmine.

OTHER FLOWERS

NEW FLOWERS

Willowherb   Campion

butterfly/bee/
hair grips

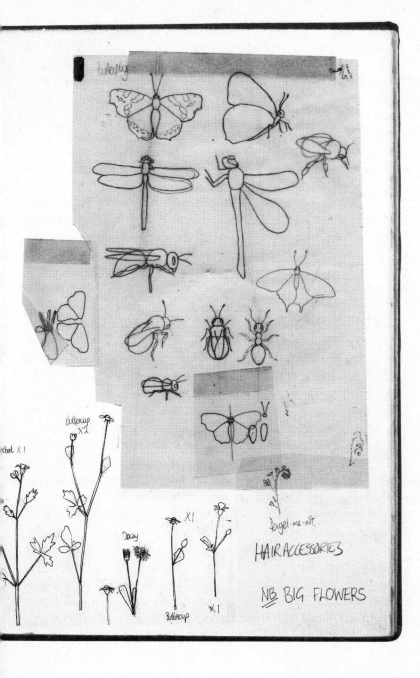

Joan was short, single, and irrepressible: a proper Scouser. Gold rings adorned her fingers, she had a gold watch on her wrist and several gold chains around her neck. Back in the good old days she had danced while the Beatles played in the Cavern and married a handsome young merchant seaman called Stan. They had three daughters together and she was promptly left to bring them up on her own, turning her hand to anything that paid the bills. Somewhere along the way she had picked up spiritual healing. Now she was in her late fifties, and still an unstoppable force,

The room was painted a dark Russian red, and I sat with the curtains drawn, a couple of nightlights flickering on the mantelpiece and the Christmas lights glowing on the tree. Joan stood behind me. I closed my eyes and did what I was told.

Relax. Focus on your breathing.

I breathed in the pine and shaken-out-match smell and listened to Joan inhaling deeply through her nose behind me. I was aware of her hands above my head, not touching me, but flat, like fans, one above the other. Then she slowly exhaled, sounding like a picture of the wind on an old map. I quickly fell into that slightly hypnotic state that I find often comes on when I'm forced to do nothing at all. It's a treat in itself, hearing everything around you more sharply than usual, almost in your sleep. Joan's breathing grew more fervent and her hands shook and vibrated above me. It was hard to keep track of time, but after some minutes, maybe ten, everything came to a kind of crescendo, with ever-faster breathing, lots of hand movements, and some other noises. Suddenly it all stopped. With a sharp exhalation of breath, Joan's hands dropped to her sides.

After a short embarrassed silence I stood up and turned on the lights.

Joan had regained her composure and was bursting to tell me all. A lot of energy, she said. She'd felt a lot of energy, and her hands had grown very hot. And then all her rings had flown off! It was remarkable. Some of them hadn't been off her fingers for years. I started scrabbling around on the floor to find them. She'd met a lot of friendly spirits on the other side – I had a lot of friends on the other side, apparently, which was reassuring – and a lot of energy. I held up the rings I'd found on the carpet. She put them back on, still full of excitement, and assured me I wouldn't be suffering from my arthritis any more. Or at least it would be much better in the future. Still on all fours, feeling about under the furniture for the last couple of rings, I thanked her from the floor. It was really very kind of her and what excellent news about the arthritis.

I found an eternity ring with a couple of stones missing, and handed it up to her, saying I felt better all ready. She looked very pleased. And then, arm stretched out full length underneath the sofa, my fingers found the last ring, still warm from Joan's hand. It was a simple gold band with three quite large diamonds set in a line, the biggest in the middle, all held in crown claw settings. It looked as if it could do with a good clean.

Slightly less than a year later Joan was lying in hospital dying from cancer. She wasn't daunted. She firmly believed in reincarnation and had already promised her daughters to return in the form of a butterfly. Towards the very end, we were all reluctant to go far from her bedside. At some point, though, Denise and her sisters disappeared for a coffee and in the dimmed light of the air-conditioned room Joan and I had a few minutes on our own. She held my hand and asked me to do something. She didn't want everyone standing around gawping at her when she died, she told me. It wasn't how she wanted to be remembered. I promised her I'd see to it.

But I'm afraid I didn't. It wasn't much longer before things started going really downhill, and as life slid away from her, I couldn't help thinking that her daughters' needs were more important than anything else now. I just couldn't bring myself to tell them her request. So in the end, I left Denise and her sisters alone with their mother, and out in the hospital corridor, I whispered Joan an apology she couldn't hear.

★

The funeral was on a crisp December day at a municipal cemetery in Kent. On our way there we all got the giggles and felt horribly guilty. The place had a conveyer-belt feel, with a queue already forming on the opposite side of the chapel for the next lot in as we left. A few days later we went to pick up the ashes. Standing under a tree in the garden of remembrance, we felt our feet shuffle and crunch on the debris of previous cremations. By this time all three girls had started to sob. Then I noticed a splash of colour on a coat. Dark orange and velvet brown, patterned with white spots. A Red Admiral had settled on Denise's shoulder. It fluttered around the three sisters, alighting on each one for a few moments, and we watched and held our breath. A butterfly so close to Christmas. It was enough to convince us all of a miracle.

Joan hadn't had much to leave. But when Denise and her sisters found the gold ring set with diamonds, the one I'd retrieved that day from under the sofa, they asked if I could do something with it. That way they could all three have a special keepsake of their mother's to treasure and pass down in turn in time. We talked, and decided on three butterfly pendants, each one set with a diamond. I'd never had a more personal commission, and probably never will.

Alongside the intimacy and individuality of this task, I found the sense of taking part in a very long tradition in the history of jewellery immensely appealing. Jewels have been handed down through the generations for centuries, repositories of wealth and emotion alike. Sometimes a setting has become damaged, or worn out, or simply looks too dated. Sometimes a collection of family jewellery has to be divided. It's an art in itself to transform an original piece into something that retains the feeling and sentiment of its past life, yet acquires new value through alteration and new ownership.

The butterflies took me a few years to make, and a good deal of that time was spent pondering over how best to approach the work. I knew that I wanted to pattern or texture the butterfly wings rather than using a filigree technique as I had before. I started experimenting with etching directly onto the silver. Usually, I'd use a sticky

214

stop-out varnish or ground to mask the areas that I didn't want the acid to erode. Detail appears when you scratch out through the stop-out. But I wanted to draw my pattern by hand this time. I felt it would connect me more directly to Joan and her beliefs, to the hand that I had held in her last days, the hand that had worn this ring for so many years.

I tried using waterproof inks in a Rotring pen. This meant I could draw fluidly and freely, and then immerse the silver in acid to erode the background. I tried several times before I was happy with my design. I decided to cut the wing shapes out in silver first, so the edges would be attacked by the acid and slightly softened. Then I watched them bubble away in the little Pyrex dish of concentrated nitric acid. After several minutes I dragged a pointer across the silver surface to feel the depth of etch, and when it was ready I ran it under the tap and washed the ink off in white spirit.

The rest was easy. I carved the body from a rod of silver, cut a piece of chenier for the diamond to sit in, and soldered it all together. I sent it to the caster's to be moulded, and cast three in 18-carat gold. When the stones were set and all polished up, and I'd chosen the right chain, I brought home three heavy golden neck-laces, a link between Denise, her sisters and their mother that would last for ever.

It's late afternoon and I'm sitting on the floor of my tiny moss-green dinghy, gently drifting along with the tide on the river Alde by Iken Cliff. She's called *Sweet Pea* and her rust-red canvas lugsail is flopping loosely from its spars. There's no hope of catching a breeze on this side of the river. Here on the southern shore you're sheltered by the trees, so I can just drift along with the tide until I reach the darker wind-ruffled water upstream, towards Snape. If I hang around I'll drift back down soon enough: the tide will soon be turning.

On a still summer's day like this, the shoreline is unrecognisable, but I'm sure I've reached the place where I saw my two turtle doves all those years ago. No swamping waves or blackening sky now, no howling wind or stinging spray. No skeleton silhouette of a blasted oak either. My tree must be gone by now. I turn my face to the sun and close my eyes and see orangey-pink and eventually I hear children's voices. My own three daughters, Verity, Connie and Libby. They've come to fetch me with Jessie, our Border collie and they're standing on the shore and calling me.

I give them a wave, settle the oars in the rowlocks and head back to shore, looking over my shoulder from time to time. The sandy cliff I remember has all but gone, eroded by tides and seasons. As soon as I'm near enough, the girls balance on grassy clumps of loamy mud and pull *Sweet Pea* in. Together we tie the lugsail to the mast, ship the oars and fasten the painter to a post with a clove hitch. We're going to walk to Snape for a pint at the Plough and Sail. As so often, we have arranged to meet my mother there, and my sister Debbie. I pull my socks and shoes on over mud-encrusted feet.

Up on the bluff by Jumbo's Cottage, I can see Denise waiting, but she's not looking at us. She's gazing out towards Iken and the church. Through the long reeds and past a couple of old boathouses, and we've soon caught her up. If there's a view that sums up Suffolk for me, it's this one. The landscape opens up to a vast expanse of mud, water, reeds and sky. Troublesome Reach, where Jumbo himself once kept the withies and marked the shifting channel. The sun picks out the northern shore a good 3 miles away. I can just about see the start of the Black Heath estate, whose land stretches down to Little Japan. But Little Japan itself is a few miles downstream, out of sight, obscured by the headland where Iken Church proudly sits. The square church tower is in full sun, nestled in oak trees on its little peninsula, the odd Scots pine dark against the sky. Out in the river, a family of seals are playing in the muddy water, and sunning themselves on the reedy islands. This is where I used to sail with Ethel and Letty, drinking Long Life beer out of tins kept cool in the bilges and released with a hiss by the sharp triangular point of a pressed-steel opener.

We carry on up the cinder track through gorse and wild plums and turn right before the Anchor, which used to be a pub when the river was busy with boatmen. Through nettles and brambles the kids walk carefully with their arms raised, sometimes stepping over and sometimes squeezing sideways to avoid a sting or a scratch. Then the path opens up and becomes soft underfoot. It's a carpet of pine needles. We're almost in a tunnel here, with pines on our left and weather-worn oaks on our right. And then out into sunshine and a field, which gently slopes up away from the river. This is a picnic area now and there are two or three cars parked up at the top end.

The river is ever present off to our right. Through a line of oak trees the thin strip of water snakes its way up to Snape, winding through the reeds with little strings of islands and lagoons ready to disorientate the inexperienced navigator. One bare-branched oak stands in isolation like a great contorted crucifix, reminding me of a necklace I made years ago. Further along, these trees grow sturdier, great grey elephant-skin trunks, around which four people couldn't link arms.

Then the track turns right, away from the rolling farmland, and back towards the river through the reeds, still within sight of the single window of the Iken Church tower, which watches us like an eye. Here there is a raised boardwalk of slatted planks covered with chicken wire for extra grip. The kids run bouncing ahead, enjoying the spring and the sound when Jessie comes racing past. Off the boardwalk, we skirt a ploughed field, soft brown and sandy, a grove of stunted oaks at its side. Up on the horizon to our left, Tunstall Forest is looking like a Colourist landscape, blocks of pink and grey and green, textured under a vast pale blue sky.

Then it's back into reed beds, another open field, and the Maltings are visible ahead of us, white chimneys behind a row of Scots pines. An oversized shire horse stands motionless in the opposite corner of the field, leaning into the harness of a cart carrying nothing but two gigantic concrete marrows. *Perceval* is a sculpture by Sarah Lucas, an oversized knick-knack of the type you used to find in a teashop window. Connie and Libby rush ahead with Jessie to climb on the horse, but Verity stops Denise and me with a hand on my arm. She has a finger raised to her lips to hush us. There's nothing to be heard but the faint swish of the breeze in the reeds. Verity points.

A massive blasted oak rises from the greenery. In its sun-bleached branches, two birds sit side by side. Not dainty turtle doves, sadly. These days they're a threatened species. The birds are bigger than collared doves too. They look like wood pigeons to me. But something about the way they sit together reminds me of that terrifying night thirty-something years ago. I look down at Verity and it's clear that the picture has captivated her. Of course, I can't tell exactly what it is that has moved her. The significance of the two birds on the branch is different for everyone who sees them. And that's just as it should be.

In the distance Jessie barks, and Connie and Libby shout to us from the horse's back.

Come on. Let's go and get that drink, I say.

Before reaching the pub, we cross over Snape Bridge. Leaning over the fence, we look down into the muddy brown estuary. It's high water. The river is perfectly smooth and calm, suspended as if holding a breath. Then we leave it behind, knowing that the tide will continue to ebb and flow, ceaselessly winding its secretive way through the reeds and past blasted oaks, where birds huddle together against the chill wind and the inevitable approaching darkness.

Acknowledgements

The biggest debt of gratitude I owe is to Lydia Syson. Without her, this book would never have happened. When I started jotting down my first doodles and formed the idea for this book, I had no idea how to go about it. My skills were firmly based in the workshop, not on the written page. Lydia took me under her wing and gently encouraged my naive haverings. She praised my infrequent successes and corrected my schoolboy errors. She taught and encouraged me until I was better able to go solo. And whenever I hit the doldrums, she patiently put me back on the right track. Lydia has been much more collaborative than an editor. Perhaps 'teacher, mentor, editor and friend' might describe her role better. However I describe her, it is because of her tireless and generous input that this book is what it is. For her intelligence, thoroughness, patience, skill, generosity and hard work, I will for ever be in her debt. A wordsmith to my goldsmith.

To my agent Jane Graham Maw for believing in me from the start.

To Helen Garnons-Williams for seeing potential in my early drafts, her astute suggestions, for giving me a chance and for all her generous support. And to all the team at Bloomsbury.

Thanks to my Mum and Dad for giving me the best ever start in life and to my amazingly generous brothers and sisters for seeing me through in one piece. Sorry you're not here to read it, Dad.

To all the gang at work for bearing the brunt of my many absences, especially to Emma.

To the kids for helping me see the familiar through youthful eyes.

And of course to my lovely wife Denise, who put up with me working all night for far too long.

A NOTE ON THE TYPE

The text of this book is set in Bembo. This type was first
used in 1495 by the Venetian printer Aldus Manutius for
Cardinal Bembo's *De Aetna*, and was cut for Manutius by
Francesco Griffo. It was one of the types used by Claude
Garamond (1480–1561) as a model for his Romain de
l'Université, and so it was the forerunner of what became
standard European type for the following two centuries. Its
modern form follows the original types and was designed
for Monotype in 1929.